Florida
CURIOSITIES

Help Us Keep This Guide Up to Date

Every effort has been made by the authors and editors to make this guide as accurate and useful as possible. However, many things can change after a guide is published— establishments close, phone numbers change, hiking trails are rerouted, facilities come under new management, etc.

We would love to hear from you concerning your experiences with this guide and how you feel it could be made better and be kept up to date. While we may not be able to respond to all comments and suggestions, we'll take them to heart and we'll also make certain to share them with the author. Please send your comments and sugges- tions to the following address:

The Globe Pequot Press
Reader Response/Editorial Department
P.O. Box 480
Guilford, CT 06437

Or you may e-mail us at:
editorial@GlobePequot.com

Thanks for your input, and happy travels!

Curiosities Series

Florida
CURIOSITIES

Quirky characters,
roadside oddities &
other offbeat stuff

Third Edition

David Grimes and Tom Becnel

Guilford, Connecticut

The prices, rates, and hours listed in this guidebook were confirmed at press time. We recommend, however, that you call establishments to obtain current information before traveling.

To buy books in quantity for corporate use or incentives, call **(800) 962–0973** or e-mail **premiums@GlobePequot.com.**

gpp®

Copyright © 2011 by Morris Book Publishing, LLC

All photos unless otherwise indicated are by the authors.

Maps by Sue Murray © Morris Book Publishing, LLC

Text design: Bret Kerr

Layout: Casey Shain

Library of Congress Cataloging-in-Publication data is available on file.

ISBN: 978-0-7627-5989-7

Printed in the United States of America

10 9 8 7 6 5 4 3 2 1

The sign reads:

LAKEWOOD FLORIDA
FLORIDA'S HIGHEST POINT
345 FT

FLORIDA DEPARTMENT OF NATURAL RESOURCES
NATIONAL PARK SERVICE
AND
LAND AND WATER CONSERVATION FUND AS COOPERATORS
WITH
WA..ON COUNTY BOARD OF COMMISSIONERS

No need for extra oxygen when visiting
Florida's highest point.

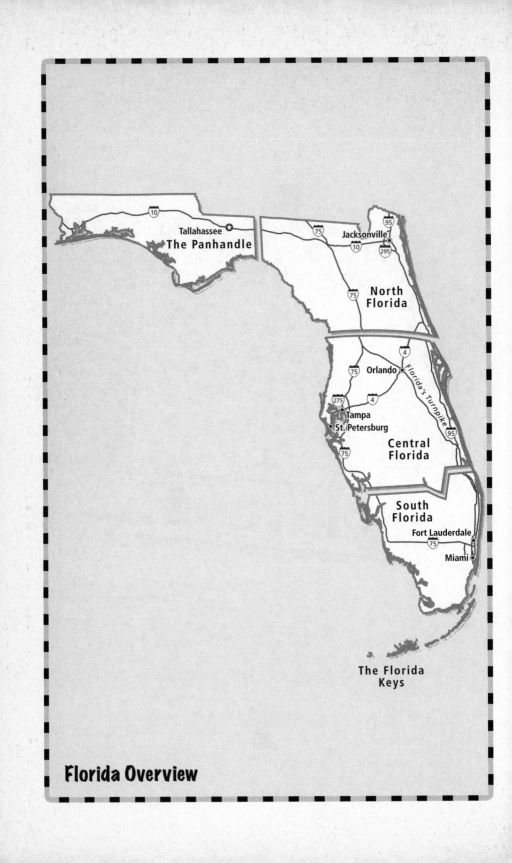

Florida Overview

contents

★ ★

introduction

*M*ost people who live in Florida came from someplace else, which either says something about the quality of life in the Sunshine State or the lack of it elsewhere. (More likely it has to do with an aversion to shoveling snow, but such a notion would put a lot of sociologists out of work.)

Florida, in a lot of ways, is an advertisement for itself. Our economy is heavily tourist-based so you hear a lot more about Disney World than you do about stingrays and no-see-ums. Florida's image is all about sunshine and sandy beaches and waterslides, all of which exist here in abundance, but they do not begin to define this wonderfully diverse state. Florida is a land of crystal-clear freshwater springs that maintain a year-round temperature of 72 degrees. Fit yourself with a snorkel and a mask and you feel like you're swimming in an aquarium. In the winter, you may find yourself sharing space with a manatee, the state's official marine mammal. They're not particularly pretty, but they're much more agreeable than most tourists.

If you like alligators, Florida is the place for you. Tourists pay to see them at roadside attractions; residents simply wait for one to crawl into

★ ★

their swimming pool, bedroom or shower stall. (We are not making this up.) The University of Florida sports teams are named, appropriately enough, the Gators. The University of Maryland sports teams, on the other hand, are named the Terps, but that is another matter for another book.

Florida is the home of the Grapefruit League, which doesn't sound all that wonderful unless you happen to be a fan of spring-training baseball. At last count (teams have a bad habit of defecting to Arizona), fifteen clubs train in Florida during the month of March. The venues are smaller and more intimate than their big-city counterparts, perhaps none cozier or more historic than McKechnie Field in Bradenton, the current spring-time home of the Pittsburgh Pirates. The St. Louis Cardinals opened play there in 1923 and there are photos of the Cards' legendary pitcher Dizzy Dean pumping gas at the station he owned in town.

Whether you come to Florida to vacation, retire or reinvent your life, you're likely to encounter many surprises. It's hot here, so it pays to hang loose and let the whole scene wash over you like a cooling July dip in Wakulla Springs.

Just watch out for the alligators.

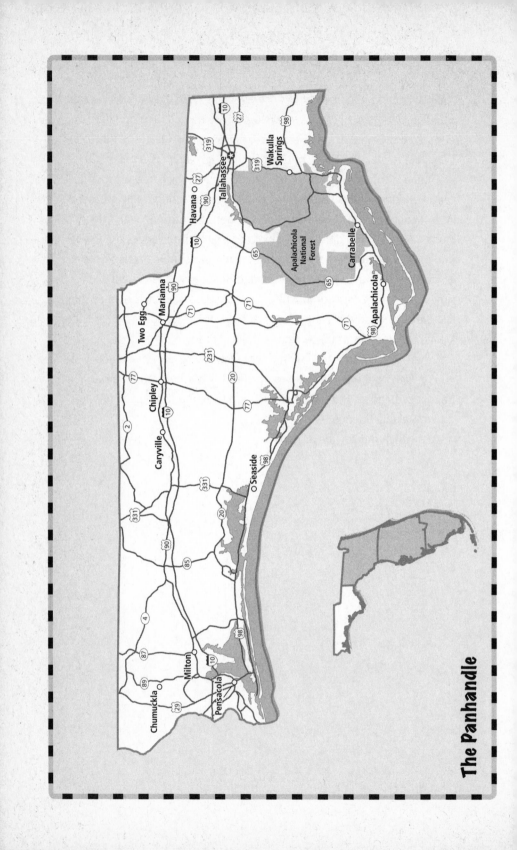

The Panhandle

1

The Panhandle

The Panhandle is *to Florida what Scotland is to Great Britain. In other words, an unwilling partner.*

The northwesternmost arm of Florida tried to quit the mother state at least twice, the most embarrassing incident occurring shortly after the Civil War when the Panhandle tried to sell itself to Alabama for $1 million, only to have the offer turned down because the Alabama legislature considered that particular tract of Florida to be a "sandbank and gopher region."

The Panhandle remains a part of Florida, but its heart and soul are way closer to Alabama and Georgia than they are to Miami, proving the old saw that the farther north you go in Florida, the more south you get. Sweet tea, grits and fried catfish continue to be staples in Panhandle cuisine, but the so-called Redneck Riviera has a lot more going for it than that. Apalachicola, on the Gulf Coast, is famous for its big, briny oysters. Nearby seaside towns entice tourists with fat, pink shrimp and succulent blue crabs. If you like seafood festivals, check out the Panhandle.

Perhaps because they consider themselves part of the Old South, Panhandle residents can be a bit contrary. Not only are most of the counties located in the Central rather than the Eastern Time Zone, the state capital, Tallahassee, is located in the Panhandle, apparently because it's an inconvenient destination for just about everyone. People here also don't tend to get as worked up as folks to the south. Spring

★ ★

break moved from Ft. Lauderdale to Panama City years ago and the locals seem to deal with the annual uproar just fine. It's probably more stoicism than tolerance, brought on by hurricanes, oil spills and just about anything man and nature can throw at you.

The western part of the Panhandle is dominated by military installations, including Eglin Air Force Base and the Pensacola Naval Air Station. The aerial sky show known as the Blue Angels practices over Pensacola Beach. If you're in the area, it's definitely a must-see. (Check times and locales at www.pensacolabeach.com/blue/.) The central part of the region is quickly becoming gentrified with the establishment of such planned communities as Seaside and Sandestin. It's a reminder that developers still rule Florida, even those parts that don't want to be a part of it. The eastern section—and most of the Panhandle, for that matter—is forest, with the exception of Tallahassee where the hot air has killed most of the trees. If you feel the need to cool off, a nice place to visit is Wakulla Springs, one of the largest and deepest freshwater springs in the world. While the 120-foot depths are murkier than they used to be, a dip in the 72-degree water is sure to clear your head, regardless of whether an alligator is eyeing you from the other shore. (For more information go to www. floridastateparks.org/wakullasprings.)

So the Panhandle is really a little piece of Florida away from Florida, a statement that probably doesn't make any sense unless you've been there.

★ ★

The Ice Man Cometh
Apalachicola

If you are able to live through a Florida summer without melting into a puddle of goo, you should give thanks to John Gorrie, the inventor of air-conditioning.

There may be some inventions we appreciate more than air-conditioning—beer springs immediately to mind—but they are hard

John Gorrie did more for Florida tourism than Walt Disney.

to imagine when you've been working outdoors in August and take that first glorious step into an air-conditioned building.

How did people live in Florida before air-conditioning? Moistly is probably the best answer.

In 1842 Gorrie, an Apalachicola medical doctor, invented refrigeration as the result of experiments to lower patients' fevers by cooling their hospital rooms. The scientific principle—heating a gas by compressing it, cooling it by sending it through radiating coils, and then expanding the gas to cool it further—is the same principle used in refrigerators and air conditioners today.

The story is that Gorrie was trying to build a machine to cool hospital rooms, but the thing kept freezing up and spewing out ice. Although Gorrie was granted the first U.S. patent for mechanical refrigeration in 1851, he never profited from it. Willis Haviland Carrier, who is often credited with inventing air-conditioning even though he only modified Gorrie's technology for commercial use sixty years later, made the money.

Gorrie's contribution to Southern living was so monumental that a museum was built in his honor in Apalachicola. Inside the one-room building is a model of his invention, which is really a primitive ice machine.

Gorrie, one of Apalachicola's pioneers, died there in 1855 at the age of fifty-one. A middle school in Jacksonville is named after him, and there is a statue of the inventor in the rotunda of the Capitol in Washington, D.C.

Pretty cool, huh?

The John Gorrie Museum is located at 46 Sixth Street in Apalachicola. The museum is open from 9:00 a.m. to 5:00 p.m. Thursday through Monday. A small admission is charged. Phone (850) 653-9347.

★ ★

Shut Up and Shuck!
Apalachicola

Believe it or not, Apalachicola, the Oyster Capital of the state, had until recently only one raw bar. That's like Kansas City having only one steak house or Seattle only one Starbucks.

But it's true. If you wanted to tuck in to some plump, salty, freshly shucked oysters tonged a few hours earlier from Apalachicola Bay, the only game in town was Boss Oyster.

A second raw bar, Papa Joe's, opened a couple of years ago, but Boss Oyster is still viewed by many as The Place. They certainly shell out the shellfish, serving ninety-four tons in a typical year in a restaurant that seats 300, according to head chef "Big" Tim Strand.

While you're sitting on the open-air deck, trying to decide which one of the five varieties of hot sauce you want to sprinkle on your oysters, you can watch the shrimp and oyster boats pull into and out of the dock. Add a colorful sunset and you might think you've died and gone to seafood-lovers' heaven.

Boss Oyster serves all kinds of seafood—crab, shrimp, scallops, grouper, you name it—but the big attraction is the oysters. Presented on a bed of cracked ice, the enormous raw shellfish are sold by the dozen, though it's the rare oyster lover who stops at twelve.

On our trip there, we got a bonus. Not only were the oysters wonderful, but we found three small pearls hiding in the shells. They weren't entirely lucky, however. Our waitress still insisted we pay the bill.

Boss Oyster is located in the Apalachicola River Inn at 125 Water Street. Phone (850) 653-9364 or log on to www.apalachicolariverinn.com.

Talk Fast, Chief, I'm Running out of Quarters
Carrabelle

The middle of the Panhandle on the Gulf of Mexico is called the Forgotten Coast because it resembles (for now) what Florida looked like before Yankee transplants and condominiums ruined everything.

★ ★

In the heart of the Forgotten Coast is Carrabelle, where somebody forgot to build a proper police station. The blue phone booth at the corner of U.S. Highway 98 and County Road 67 has been described as the World's Smallest Police Station. What many people don't realize is that when the phone booth was erected in 1963, it was an improvement over the old police communications facility, a phone on the wall across the street.

"Every time it rained, the man who answered the phone would get wet," said former police chief Jesse Smith.

When he was not patrolling, Smith parked by the phone booth. "We'd just sit there because there was a little shade and it's right in the middle of town. We could see everything that was going on, and if people needed to get ahold of us, they'd call and we'd answer the phone." (You could ring up the police station/phone booth then by dialing 3691. Phone number prefixes were apparently another forgotten thing in Carrabelle.)

In 1991, Smith told Johnny Carson all about the World's Smallest Police Station on the *Tonight Show,* and the little cop shop was also featured on *Real People.* Today, visitors from around the world visit Carrabelle to have their picture taken next to the police booth, which was replaced years ago by a more conventional police station that late-night comedians have thus far ignored. In fact, there's no longer even a phone in the booth, thanks in part to tourists making unauthorized long-distance calls and college students trying to steal the whole package. (They were caught, and the phone booth was returned to its rightful place. Just because they work out of a phone booth doesn't mean Carrabelle police aren't alert.)

Today, you might find a Carrabelle patrol car parked in the vicinity of the tiny old police station, but visitors who want more information about the history of the thing would be better off popping into Carrabelle Realty next door, where transplanted Brit Rene Topping is glad to answer questions and offer up anecdotes, including the one about the 300-pound deputy who was too fat to squeeze inside the phone booth.

★ ★

About the size of a phone booth, this police station is
occasionally stolen by college students.

From her we learned that Carrabelle, a working man's village of
1,400 souls devoted mostly to commercial fishing, once played an
important role in World War II by serving as a huge military training
facility. More than 30,000 troops were stationed here and on nearby
Dog Island in an assemblage of 1,100 buildings called Camp Gordon
Johnston. There was a bombing range, a bazooka range, a bayonet
and knife course, and what would surely be our least favorite obstacle, a series of shell holes and trenches where machine guns would
fire live ammunition just 30 inches above the ground while troops
crawled underneath.

Hello? Carrabelle police? Is anyone there? HELP!!!

Worm Fiddlin'
Caryville

If you fiddle, they will come.

The "they" in this case is worms. Big fat night crawlers. Lots of 'em.

Jack and JoAn Palmer of the Panhandle town of Caryville held the town's first worm fiddlin' festival in 1976 as part of Florida's U.S. Bicentennial Celebration. Usually held over the Labor Day weekend, the festival has been cancelled on several occasions due to floods or drought. Either way, the tradition of worm fiddlin', which is most definitely a Southern thing, lives on. JoAn said she and a friend once fiddled up 205 worms in five minutes in a 6-by-6-foot square of ground. That's a lot of fish bait.

Mrs. Palmer explained the art of worm fiddlin' this way:

"You take a sharpened two-by-four and hammer it into the ground with the back of an ax. Then you run the blade of the ax up and down the board so it makes an eh-eh-eh sound."

The eh-eh-eh sound does not translate well in the printed word, but apparently to worms' ears, assuming worms have ears, it sounds like the music in the shower scene of *Psycho*.

"One boy stuck a truck spring in the ground and ran his ax over it," Mrs. Palmer continued. "It's the vibration that brings the worms up."

Worm fiddling, sometimes called snoring worms, is practiced throughout the South, but Caryville might be the only place that chose to make it the centerpiece of an annual festival. Most every Labor Day, people would come from miles around to watch Mrs. Palmer, her husband, Jack, and anyone else with an ax to grind fiddle up some worms. There was always music and plenty of food. (No worm burgers, however.)

The festival took a nosedive after the big flood of 1994 when the Choctawhatchee River overflowed its banks and inundated the tiny town. The Palmers, who had 4 feet of water in their living room, were one of the few families who chose to stay, rebuilding their house on higher ground. The last Worm Fiddling Festival was in 1996, but Mrs. Palmer isn't ruling out a comeback.

"If enough people show an interest, we'll do it again, I guess," she said.

Until such time, her fiddlin' record of 205 worms in five minutes should be safe.

Caryville is located off Interstate 10 about 8 miles west of Bonifay.

Breaking off the Panhandle

The Panhandle region of Florida, extending west nearly to Mobile, Alabama, is more Southern than south Florida. There are more young natives and fewer northern retirees. More grits and fewer bagels. The drawls can be as thick as those grits, and the Civil War is still sometimes referred to as simply "the wah."

The Florida capital is part of the Panhandle, but state representatives from Miami are closer to Havana than they are to Tallahassee. If the southeastern United States made geographical sense, Florida's capital would be near Orlando, and the Panhandle would be part of Alabama. What's almost forgotten in state history is that this division almost happened after the Civil War. Florida offered to sell the territory to Alabama. The war-depleted Cotton State couldn't come up with the money, so the Panhandle coastline, now known as "The Redneck Riviera," remained a part of Florida.

The Kudzu Also Rises
Chipley

You see it everywhere in the South, climbing trees and utility poles, wrapping itself around sheds and abandoned cars, blanketing the landscape like a lush green quilt.

Kudzu is the polite name for it. Less flattering names include cuss you, the foot-a-night vine, and the vine that ate the South. That last characterization is not far from wrong: Kudzu covers seven million acres in the Deep South and would surely cover more if people weren't working so hard to get rid of the fast-growing weed.

Kudzu did not always have a bad reputation. You could say it grew into it. The oriental vine was first introduced to this country in 1876 when the Japanese used it to shade their exhibit booth at the U.S. Centennial Exposition in Philadelphia. The idea caught on, and people from Virginia to Alabama began planting the stuff as a porch vine.

Enter Charles E. and Lillie Pleas, a kindly Quaker couple who had relocated from Indiana to tiny Chipley in northwest Florida. Both naturalists, the Pleas discovered that animals would eat the plant, so they began promoting its use as forage in the 1920s. Their Glen Arden Nursery sold kudzu plants through the mail. A historical marker on the site of the old nursery, now the Washington County Agricultural Center on U.S. Highway 90, proudly proclaims KUDZU DEVELOPED HERE.

During the Great Depression of the 1930s, the Soil Conservation Service promoted kudzu for erosion control. (Its very ability to hold soil in place is what makes it so hard to kill; kudzu's roots can extend 8 feet into the earth.) Hundreds of young men were given work planting kudzu through the Civilian Conservation Corps. Farmers were paid as much as eight dollars an acre as incentive to plant fields of the vines in the 1940s.

The problem with kudzu is that it grows too well, smothering native crops and plants and covering trees so densely that they die for lack of light. The vine can grow as quickly as a foot a day, and some herbicides actually make it grow faster. After the USDA declared

* *

kudzu a weed in 1972, it's all been pretty much downhill for the vine ever since.

While there are many who wish the Pleas had been a little less successful in promoting kudzu, the plant is not universally hated. Basket makers do great things with the rubberlike vines, a South Carolina woman makes paper from kudzu, and you can find kudzu blossom jelly, kudzu syrup, kudzu burgers, even kudzu wine. (We'll just have a Coke, thank you.)

There are several kudzu festivals around the Southeast, but none, sadly, in Chipley, the adopted home of kudzu pioneers Charles and Lillie Pleas.

"I guess a lot of people around here would just as soon keep quiet about that," said former Chipley mayor Tommy McDonald.

The marker commemorating the achievement (abomination) of Charles and Lillie Pleas is located in front of the Washington County Agricultural Center on US 90 in downtown Chipley. The Pleas are buried in the Glenwood Cemetery on Glenwood Avenue. Their side-by-side graves, about two-thirds of the way back, on the right, are marked by a tombstone that reads KUDZU PIONEERS.

Who You Callin' a Redneck?
Chumuckla

The Chumuckla Redneck Parade got its start in 1994 when some good old boys got into the Jack Daniel's on Christmas Eve and had to be led home by their wives. Some parade, somewhere, has probably been inspired by less, but we can't think of one offhand.

"It started as a joke," said parade founder Kathy Barr, "but it caught on and kept growing."

Today, nearly 10,000 people come from as far away as Dothan, Alabama, and Fort Walton Beach to watch or participate in the Redneck Parade, which is held every year on the second Sunday in December.

(Continued on page 14)

Against All Odds

The Seminole is the only tribe of American Indians that never signed a peace treaty with the United States.

Fat lot of good it did them.

Calling themselves the "Unconquered People," the Florida tribe was reduced to fewer than 300 people after three wars with the United States between 1817 and 1858. At one point, 3,000 poorly armed warriors were pitted against four U.S. generals and more than 200,000 troops. This, the Second Seminole War (1835–1842), was the fiercest and most expensive war ever waged by the U.S. government against Native Americans. The low point came in 1837 when Gen. Thomas Jesup, flying a truce flag, lured the great Seminole leader Osceola into a trap. Captured, Osceola was shipped off to prison at Fort Moultrie, near Charleston, South Carolina, where he died a year later.

By 1858, after years of war, more than 3,000 Seminoles had been uprooted and relocated west of the Mississippi, mostly in Oklahoma. One of them was Billy Bowlegs, the Seminole leader in the Third Seminole War (1855–1858). Bowlegs and his war-weary band surrendered on May 7, 1858, after the U.S. government promised him a substantial amount of money for his land. Thirty-eight warriors and eighty-five women and children, including Billy's wife, boarded the steamer *Grey Cloud* at Egmont Key, south of Tampa, to begin their journey to Indian territory in what is now Oklahoma. Billy was never compensated, and he died on April 27, 1859, after a brief stint in the Union Army.

Things didn't begin to turn around for the Seminoles until 1970, when the Indian Claims Commission awarded the Seminoles (of both Oklahoma and Florida) $12,347,500 for the land taken from them by the U.S. military. The Seminole tribe was recognized as an entity separate from the State of Florida and the United States. In 1977, the Seminoles opened the first tax-free "smoke shop," selling discount cigarettes and tobacco products. The opening of the tribe's first high-stakes bingo hall in Hollywood was a national first, and gaming has since become the largest single source of revenue for Native Americans.

Today, more than 2,000 descendants of the last 300 Florida Seminoles live on six reservations in the state: Hollywood, Big Cypress, Brighton, Immokalee, Fort Pierce, and Tampa.

The Seminole canoe has been replaced by cars, airplanes, and airboats, and instead of telling stories around the fire, Seminoles, like most modern Americans, prefer to watch TV.

The county of Osceola, near Disney World in east central Florida, was named after the Indian leader. Micanopy (pronounced *mick-a-NO-pee*), a town in Alachua County popular with antiques hunters, is named after the Seminole leader of the Second Seminole War. His name translates to "top chief." Okeechobee, the huge lake in south central Florida, comes from the Seminole for "big water."

There are at least five Florida sports teams called the Seminoles, not the least of which is the FSU Seminoles, based at Florida State University in Tallahassee. Many other Florida town and place names have Seminole roots.

★ ★

(Continued from page 11)

It's easy to participate in the Redneck Parade, but before you sign up, it would probably be a good idea to go out and buy yourself a set of Bubba Teeth. Bubba Teeth, for those of you who are unfamiliar with the things (that would include us, until Kathy Barr filled us in), are splayed, discolored fake choppers with more than a few gaps. Think of the dental work of the hillbillies in *Deliverance* and you've got a pretty good picture. Bubba Teeth are, needless to say, available in all of the finer convenience stores in and around Chumuckla.

Feel free to create your own redneck-themed float. A popular one in a past parade was Santa Claus in a bathtub pulled by a go-kart. (No, we weren't aware Santa Claus was a redneck either. The Redneck Parade is nothing if not instructive.)

And no Florida celebration, festival, or parade would be complete without some sort of beauty pageant, or in this case, lack-of-beauty pageant. Folks from miles around vie for the titles of King and Queen Redneck.

Chumuckla is located about 25 miles northeast of Pensacola on County Road 182. Don't blink or you'll miss it; there's not even so much as a traffic light. Proceeds benefit the Chumuckla Athletic Association. For more information on the Redneck Parade, call the Santa Rosa County Chamber of Commerce at (850) 623-2339.

Nobody Named Fidel Here

Havana

Havana, Florida, is not the kind of town you're likely to stumble upon while celebrating spring break or motoring toward Disney World. Located in the Panhandle, Havana is a predominantly African-American suburb of Tallahassee, the state's capital. Boasting a population of about 1,800, Havana borders Georgia in Gadsden County and is known nowadays for its art and antiques shops. Back in the day (we're talking the early 1900s), Havana was a big part of Florida's cigar industry. A plant called "shade tobacco" grew well in Havana and other parts of Gadsden County. The leaves formed the wrappings of premium Florida cigars.

That's probably history enough for a small Panhandle town, but according to www.visitgadsden.com, Havana also has a clay-like soil that became the basis for kitty litter. Furthermore, it has a disproportionate number of people who became rich by investing in Coca-Cola stock.

So there.

When Love Is in the Air
Marianna

If you drive through Florida in May or September, you might notice—no, you definitely will notice—that the air is thick with some sort of slow-moving black fly. Then you will notice that the flies make no effort to get out of the way, and your windshield (not to mention your headlights, grille, and radiator) is soon covered by a thick layer of sticky gore.

This is how most people are first introduced to love bugs, so named because the male and the female of the species fly around in love's embrace, hoping to end their lives Romeo-and-Juliet style on the windshield of a passing Oldsmobile.

The bane of motorists and the boon of car washes, love bugs do not sting or bite or carry any diseases. They just make love (preferably over highways; they're attracted by auto exhaust) until the smaller male drops off dead or the tandem splats against a windshield, whichever comes first. They lead a rather one-dimensional life, love bugs.

Your average Floridian is a lot more familiar with love bugs than he is with swamp cabbage or manatees or conchs, so it was just a matter of time before somebody came up with the idea of a Love Bug Festival.

That man is Ted Eubanks, and his celebration of the bug of love takes place the first weekend in June at the fairgrounds in Marianna.

★ ★

There is the usual assortment of arts and crafts, food vendors, sack races, and pony rides, but the highlight of the festival is the crowning of Little Miss Love Bug.

We asked Ted if Little Miss Love Bug celebrates her victory by killing Little Mister Love Bug or by pasting herself on the windshield of a passing VW Beetle. Happily (or sadly, depending on how sick you are), Miss Love Bug does neither. She simply thanks the judges and then moseys off for a funnel cake and maybe some ribs.

Ted says he hopes to add more love-buggy elements to future festivals, including a costume parade.

"About all we have now is a 2-inch-by-2-inch love bug house," he says. "Love bugs could fly in there if they wanted to, but so far they haven't."

Marianna is located about 60 miles northwest of Tallahassee off US 90. For more information about the Love Bug Festival, call (850) 526-7777.

Itching to Have a Party
Milton

Back in the good old days, before the invention of insect repellent or a decent pair of wading boots, the pioneers who founded the Panhandle town of Milton had to slog through the marshes and swamps of the Blackwater River. The mucky trek resulted in numerous mosquito bites, not to mention briar and sandspur scratches to the ankle and leg. It must have been bad, because the pioneers began calling themselves Scratch Ankles, a nickname that residents of Milton continue to use to this day.

Of course nothing is official until you have a celebration in its honor, which explains the Scratch Ankle Festival held every spring in Milton for the past thirty years. There aren't any contests involving barefoot runs through briar patches, but you can gorge on hot dogs and funnel cakes and listen to local bands play country music and gospel. The highlight of the event, which usually takes place in late March, is the coronation of Little Mr. and Miss Scratch Ankle, a pageant open only to couples between the ages of four and six. It is, needless to say, unbearably cute and, we understand, quite competitive.

No word on whether there is a runner-up that can step up to serve the remainder of the term if the winning couple is unable to fulfill their duties, whatever they may be. Learning the alphabet, perhaps.

The Scratch Ankle Festival is held in Milton on North and South Willing Streets. For more information call (850) 626-6246 or visit www.mainstreetmilton.org.

Why Drive When You Can Fly?
Pensacola

Pensacola has been dubbed "The Cradle of Naval Aviation" for good reason.

The world's first naval air station was built in this Panhandle town in 1914, and today Pensacola is the home of the Blue Angels precision flying team and the equally impressive National Naval Aviation Museum.

After World War II, Admiral Chester Nimitz ordered the formation of a precision flying team to maintain the public's interest in naval aviation. The team was almost named the Blue Lancers until a pilot saw a magazine advertisement for a New York nightclub called the Blue Angel. Flying a variety of ever-faster Navy fighter jets, the Blue Angels have awed and entertained over 300 million spectators at air shows dating back to 1946.

From March through November you can watch the Blue Angels practice at Pensacola Naval Air Station's Sherman Field. The free exhibitions are held Tuesday and Wednesday mornings (weather permitting) and give you a chance to get an up-close look as the pilots of the mighty blue-and-gold F/A-18 Hornets perform their death-defying acrobatics just a few feet above the tarmac. For more information about the show, visit www.blueangels.navy.mil/.

★ ★

After watching the Blue Angels, it's a short stroll to the National Naval Aviation Museum. More than 150 old and new aircraft are on display here, and there's also a full-size replica of a World War II aircraft carrier flight deck. If your stomach is strong, crawl into the IMAX flight simulator to find out what it feels like to take off in a Hornet, fly at over 150 miles per hour, and land on the deck of a carrier. For details go to www.navalaviationmuseum.org.

For the less adventuresome, we recommend a visit to nearby Santa Rosa Island. The beaches are soft and white, and the sunsets are very easy on the stomach.

"UFO House" Draws Double-takes
Pensacola Beach

In 1970, a spaceship landed on Pensacola Beach. The saucer-shaped vessel perched atop a conventional cinder-block structure, which made it all the more striking to drivers passing Panferio Drive. The elliptical windows that ring the saucer appear as alien eyes surveying the Panhandle landscape. Soon this spaceship had a nickname: "the UFO House."

Thousands of visitors to Pensacola Beach take pictures of the house. In the summer height of tourist season, neighbors expect a constant stream of sunburned photographers. A trip to the beach wouldn't be complete without a double- or triple-take at the most remarkable house in Santa Rosa County.

The fiberglass spaceship was built as a mass-produced Futuro home designed by Finnish architect Matti Suuronen. Its 600 square feet of space includes a bedroom, bath, kitchen and living area. The ramp rising up the rear of the ship recalls *The Day the Earth Stood Still,* a 1951 science-fiction movie.

The UFO House has survived several hurricanes. Different local people have lived in the home. It's also been open for rent.

For Halloween, it's often open to trick-or-treaters. Sometimes it's draped in orange, like a great pumpkin. Other times, it's just a house shaped like a flying saucer, perfect for guests dressed like aliens.

This Futuro house delights visitors to Pensacola Beach.

The "Chic Mayberry" of the Panhandle
Seaside

The Panhandle resort town of Seaside, a model home for "New Urbanism" in Florida, served as a backdrop for the 1996 Jim Carrey movie *The Truman Show*. To express a vision of ersatz Americana, producers needed a super-stereotypical small town with brick streets, picket fences, and everything within easy walking distance. Seaside fit the bill.

After filming ended, a few fake storefronts were left standing for a while, because founder Robert Davis liked the way they looked. This says a little something about the genuine unreality of Seaside.

Decorative gazebos mark beach access in the
Panhandle community of Seaside, Florida.

Davis, along with architects Andres Duany and Elizabeth Plater-Zyberk, built Seaside on a gorgeous stretch of Panhandle coastline in 1982. It was a revelation in urban planning, receiving universal acclaim for being pedestrian-friendly, promoting bold colors and metal roofs, and banning lawns in favor of natural landscaping.

What was planned as a modest community, however, quickly became a weekend getaway for the wealthy citizens of Montgomery and Birmingham, New Orleans and Atlanta. And now the quiet coastal highway is jammed with Seaside imitators and anti-Seaside sprawl.

For a twentieth-anniversary story, the *Palm Beach Post* called Seaside a "chic Mayberry." Others aren't so kind. Detractors who'd like to hate the place need look no further than the oh-so-cutesy name of a Seaside trinket shop: Sue Vaneers.

How a Panhandle Town Was Hatched
Two Egg

With the Pittman grocery long closed, and the crumbling old Hart store scheduled to be demolished, the Lawrence Grocery Store remains the heart and soul of Two Egg, Florida, a crossroads town northeast of Marianna. The sagging wood-frame building provides a single Chevron gas pump and sells candy bars and plumbing fixtures, cigarettes and car batteries, *Florida Farmer* magazine and the *Jackson County News*. Nell King, the native who bought the store in 1990, knows everyone in town, which isn't that hard, considering the local population.

"It's probably about thirty-two; that's what it says on the sign," she says. "We have to count 'em up if someone dies or moves out."

King lives next door to the grocery store in a small house behind a big oak tree. The license plate on her car reads two egg 1. Her husband, of course, is two egg 2. Back at the store, some of the most popular items for sale are Two Egg souvenirs.

(Continued on page 24)

Way Down Upon the Racist Lyrics

The Suwannee is a scenic 250-mile river that meanders south from Okeefenokee Swamp in Georgia to the Gulf of Mexico, forming (more or less) the eastern boundary of the Florida Panhandle. However pretty it may be, the Suwannee was just another river until it was made famous by the 1851 hit single, "Swanee River," also known as "Old Folks at Home."

The river's big break almost never happened. Composer Stephen Foster originally chose South Carolina's Pee Dee River as the song's namesake. Foster wisely decided that the lyric "way down upon the Pee Dee River" might not capture the public's imagination; after consulting an atlas, he settled on the far more mellifluous Suwannee.

The atlas was as close as Foster ever came to the Suwannee, or to Florida for that matter. Born in Pittsburgh in 1826, Foster spent his entire life in the North, where he became the most prolific and successful songwriter of his day. It's too bad they didn't have greatest-hits albums back in those days, because Foster's would have been a monster. Besides "Old Folks at Home," he penned "Beautiful Dreamer," "Camptown Races," "Jeanie with the Light Brown Hair," "Oh! Susanna," "My Old Kentucky Home," and, as they like to say on the late-night commercials, "many, many more."

Foster is to be credited—or blamed—for launching Florida's tourist industry. "Swanee River" sold hundreds of thousands of copies, and, starting in the late 1800s, folks from Up North began coming to Florida, seeking the quaint, happy plantation world that Foster made up for the purposes of his song. The tune had such an impact that the Florida legislature made it the official state song in 1935. Unfortunately, the lyrics of "Swanee River" have become a tad—how shall we say?—dated. To put it another way, it's not the first song we'd choose to sing at our next Kwanzaa party. Here's how the original lyrics begin:

Way down upon de Swanee Ribber,
Far, far away,
Dere's wha my heart is turning ebber,
Dere's wha de old folks stay.
All up and down de whole creation
Sadly I roam,
Still longing for de old plantation,
And for de old folks at home.
All de world am sad and dreary,
Eb-rywhere I roam;
Oh, darkeys, how my heart grows weary,
Far from de old folks at home!

Perhaps to prevent a riot, the word "brothers" was substituted for "darkeys" when the song was sung at the dedication of the new Florida capitol building in 1978. Modern published versions of the song also eliminate the dialect.

Maybe everyone would have been better off if Florida had stuck with its original state song, adopted in 1913 and titled "Florida, My Florida." Written in 1894 by Rev. Dr. C. V. Waugh, a professor of languages at the Florida Agricultural College at Lake City, the song was said by the legislature to have "both metric and patriotic merit of the kind calculated to inspire love for home and native State." Sung to the tune of "Maryland, My Maryland," one verse goes like this:

The golden fruit the world outshines
Florida, my Florida
Thy gardens and thy phosphate mines
Florida, my Florida.

Ah, yes. What Floridian's eyes don't get a little misty thinking about those lovely phosphate mines? "Swanee River" has its faults, granted, but at least it doesn't ask us to get nostalgic over some big ugly holes in the ground.

(Continued from page 21)

There are Two Egg caps, T-shirts, and sweatshirts. Two Egg greeting cards and Two Egg license plates. Two Egg paintings by Marian Oswald of nearby Bascom, Florida. Finally, there's Two Egg cane syrup made by Robert E. Long, another native of the town—"a Two Egg-ian," says King, who is used to customers asking questions.

"We have visitors from everywhere, reporters from everywhere," she told us. "Our sign's the most replaced sign in Florida." People steal it all the time.

The folksy name of Two Egg, of course, continues to draw curious tourists and tour groups. There are several versions of the story about how the town was named. Most involve a farm boy trading eggs for candy.

Dick Hinson, an amateur historian of Jackson County, offers to cut through the confusion. "About a hundred years ago, let's say 1910, a traveling salesman—we used to call 'em drummers—was calling on the general store," Hinson says. "A little boy came in with two eggs, and was given a choice of candy from the counter. When the store owner said he was going to name the town, the drummer said he ought to call it Two Egg."

Me Tarzan, You Jane
Wakulla Springs

We will resist the temptation to call the waters of Wakulla Springs "gin clear," as it has been our experience that the stuff makes things less clear rather than more. Suffice it to say that the water here is really, really clear. If the light is right, you can see things on the bottom, 185 feet down. In 1850, a woman reportedly spotted the bones of a mastodon at the bottom of the springs. No word on whether gin was involved.

Located about 30 miles south of Tallahassee, Wakulla Springs is the focal point of the Edward Ball Wakulla Springs State Park and Lodge. One of the largest and deepest freshwater springs in the world,

★ ★

Wakulla Springs is fed by an underground river that gushes water at the rate of 400,000 gallons a minute. Divers entering the mouth of the underwater cavern often have their face masks blown off by the force of the current. (Spring Creek Spring, also in Wakulla County, is the state's biggest gusher, emitting 1.3 *billion* gallons of sparkling clear water a day. Take that, Perrier.)

Florida has about 200 freshwater springs, all of them beautiful, but there are several things that make Wakulla unique. For starters, no one has ever discovered the source of the spring. In 1989, a professional cave-diving expedition into the springs was filmed for a *National Geographic* television special. Other professional dive teams have traveled more than a mile and descended more than 300 feet into the honeycomb of limestone caves beneath the springs. At that point, the cavern branches into four channels, each tunneling still deeper into the earth. That's as far as anyone's gotten.

Wakulla Springs is also a popular hangout for slimy manlike creatures with gills and webbed feet. The movie *The Creature from the Black Lagoon* was filmed here, as were several early Tarzan movies starring Johnny Weissmuller (the only *real* Tarzan, as far as we're concerned), *Airport '77,* and the unforgettable *Joe Panther.*

The last thing that makes Wakulla Springs unique is the lodge. The twenty-seven-room retreat was built in 1937 by Edward Ball, entrepreneur, financier, railroad magnate, and owner of a big chunk of property surrounding the springs. Listed on the National Register of Historic Places, the lodge is a symphony of hand-wrought iron, marble, and imported handmade ceramic tile. But that's not the unique part. The unique part is that there are no televisions in the rooms! That's right, folks. Consider this before making reservations.

Otherwise, Wakulla is just your typical, otherworldly gorgeous Florida spring. The 75-degree waters are a bit of a shock, even on the hottest summer day. There's a 15-foot-high diving platform if you want to get it over with right away, or you can do it like we do and inch in a bit at a time, flapping your arms and yelling,

★ ★

"OhmigodIt'sCold!" Once in, you'll be swimming over, around, and with many species of freshwater fish, including bass, catfish, and bream. And don't be surprised if you see the occasional alligator. Hey, it's Florida.

Wakulla Springs is located off State Road 363 about 30 miles south of Tallahassee. There is a $6 admission charge to enter the park. Glass-bottom boat tours are available for an additional fee. For more information or to make reservations, contact Edward Ball Wakulla Springs State Park at (850) 926-0700 or visit online at www.florida stateparks.org/WAKULLASPRINGS/.

The Possum Monument
Wausau

Wausau, a small town south of Chipley, which is a small town west of Tallahassee, staked its claim to fame in 1982. That's when Panhandle community leaders got the Florida Legislature to designate the first Saturday in August as "Possum Day." On that summer weekend, locals and visitors began gathering in Washington County to celebrate an annual "Funday and Possum Festival."

Near the intersection of State Road 77 and County Road 278, Wausau raised a massive granite monument with a pseudo-serious inscription:

"Erected in grateful recognition of the role of the North American possum, a magnificent survivor of the marsupial family pre-dating the ages of the mastodon and the dinosaur, has played in furnishing both food and fur for the early settlers and their successors. Their presence here has provided a source of nutritious and flavorful food in normal times and has been important aid to human survival in times of distress and critical need."

The annual celebration features a parade, auction and concert, along with hundreds of people posing for souvenir photos at the Possum Monument. For the rest of the year, it's a lonely chunk of rock on the side of a quiet road. Across the street is a Tom Thumb convenience store. Debora Cooper, a clerk at the store, could see the monument from her counter if she bothered to look.

"I don't pay any attention to it," she says with a shrug, "but I think it's pretty cool."

In Wausau, possum-lovers make pilgrimages
to a granite monument.

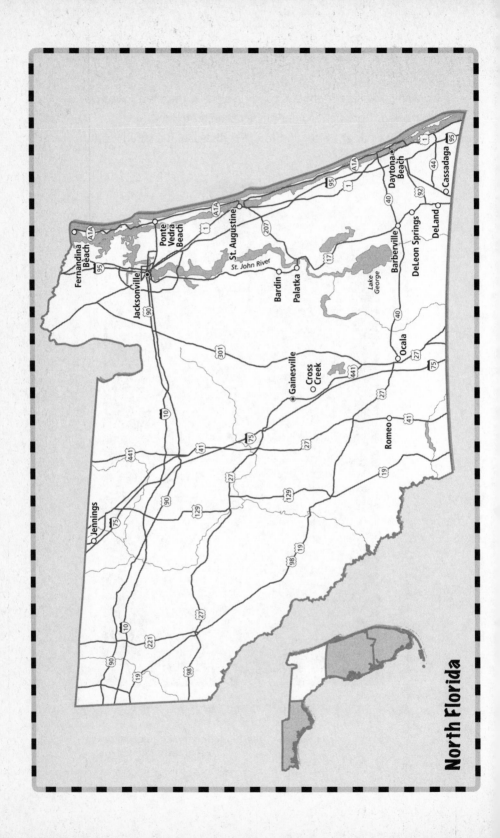

North Florida

2

North Florida

North Florida may *sound like an oxymoron, but in reality it is history that defines this diverse region.*

In 1513, Juan Ponce de León set out from Puerto Rico to the Bahamas in search of the fabled Fountain of Youth. León would have benefitted from a modern GPS because he missed his destination by a wide margin and wound up landing near present-day St. Augustine. Impressed with the new land's beautiful flowers, Ponce de León named his discovery La Florida, meaning "festival of flowers," and claimed it in the name of the king of Spain. So Ponce de León never found his Fountain of Youth, but he did "discover" Florida, so his trip was not a total loss. (There is a Fountain of Youth tourist attraction in modern-day St. Augustine and you can begin planning your trip there by going to www.fountainofyouthflorida.com.)

Up the coast a ways is Fernandina Beach, which also reeks of history. You can visit the museum or the fort, but our favorite activity is the pub crawl, which takes you through four historic taverns including the Palace Saloon (www.palacesaloon.com), Florida's oldest continuously operating drinking establishment. The Palace's specialty is a rum concoction called Pirate's Punch. A couple of these and you might see Ponce de León's ghost wandering the premises.

After you sober up, you might want to visit nearby Jacksonville, Florida's largest city (in area) and a place dear to the heart of (who knew?) Elvis. Between 1955 and 1977, the year he died, The King did seventeen shows here, which could qualify Jacksonville as the pelvis-gyrating capital of the world. In his later years, Elvis liked to stay at the downtown Hilton Hotel. You can visit his favorite room (if nobody's occupying it) and try to imagine hordes of teenage girls screaming your name ten stories below your window. Or you can just take a picture and leave, which is probably a more sensible thing to do.

Daytona Beach is south of St. Augustine and home not only to the Daytona 500 stock car race but also Bike Week, an event apparently designed for people who don't find the race crazy enough. You definitely want to bring your camera to this shindig. Leather chaps wouldn't be a bad idea, either.

The Big Bend area of North Florida is directly to the west on the Gulf Coast. It's a great place to go if you're a seafood lover or an avid fisherman. The pace is much slower here than on the east coast, the beaches have better sand and the people hardly ever look at you funny unless you order something other than sweet iced tea with your grouper sandwich.

★ ★

Give Us Your Tired, Your Hungry, Your Huddled Carousel Horses Yearning to Breathe Free

Barberville

If you're in the market for a cast aluminum Statue of Liberty—and who isn't these days?—the place to go is Barberville Produce at the corner of State Road 17 and State Road 40 in, needless to say, Barberville. It may be the only place in America where you can buy a suit of armor and a bag of boiled peanuts at the same time.

Barberville Produce is about all there is to Barberville. At the very least, it's the town's most conspicuous aspect. To say you can't miss it is an understatement. The owner, David Biggers, claims to have a million items strewn about the roadside property. That might be an exaggeration, but not by much. There is stuff of every description and in quantities too numerous to count. Besides the aforementioned Statues of Liberty, there are carousel horses, streetlights, fountains, giant clocks, skulls of longhorn cattle, dancing gators, and innumerable ceramic frogs.

"We have a little bit of this and a little bit of that," says Biggers modestly.

Biggers doesn't make the stuff himself ("That's the first question everyone asks me"); he just sells it. If it doesn't sell, it doesn't stay.

"I don't deal in dead horses," he says.

If true, that's about the only thing he doesn't deal in.

Biggers doesn't put price tags on his merchandise because, as he likes to say, "This is not Wal-Mart."

Few people would confuse the two. With its cardboard-covered walkways and jumbled merchandise, Barberville Produce is more like a flea market, only with weirder stuff.

Though it's rather hard to believe by the looks of the place, Biggers says he sells mostly to "upscale" customers looking to enhance the looks of their property with a giant, three-tiered, cast aluminum fountain or a carousel horse. Restaurants and other businesses "trying to attract attention" buy the Statues of Liberty and suits of armor, and

★ ★

municipalities buy the ornate street lamps to spruce up their business districts.

If you're not in the market for a cattle skull or giant clock, you can buy some fresh fruits and vegetables at the adjoining produce stand.

We highly recommend the boiled peanuts.

Barberville Produce is located at 141 West Highway 40. Hours are 9:00 a.m. to 6:00 p.m., and they are open seven days a week. Phone (386) 749-3562.

If you're shopping for a Statue of Liberty—or seven—to embellish your front lawn, Barberville Produce is the place to go.

✦ ✦

That's Mr. Booger to You

Bardin

Let other states brag about their Bigfoot, Sasquatch, or Abominable Snowman. In northeast Florida, the only mythical hairy monster worth talking about is the Bardin Booger.

Bardin is an almost nonexistent town northwest of Palatka. There used to be a sign on County Road 209A informing motorists that they were entering Bardin, but a car knocked it over a couple of years ago and nobody bothered to put up a new one. The hub, if it can be called that, of Bardin is Bud's Grocery, which used to be the focal point of all things Booger. Old-timers would sit on the front porch of Bud's and discuss the comings and goings of the Booger as casually as people in other towns might talk about the weather. One old boy claimed he saw the Booger running through the woods, carrying a lantern. Another said he saw him snatching laundry off a clothesline. Still another swore he surprised the Booger while the creature was peering in the refrigerator, looking for a snack.

The Booger has made itself scarce for about the past forty years, leading some to speculate that it either died or moved to a place less populated, like maybe Mars. (Actually, the new home of the Booger is believed to be Welatka, an even less wide place in the road south of Bardin.)

Today, all that is left of the legend is Lena Crain, a perky, diminutive, seventy-one-year-old Palatka woman who tends the Booger's flame—or lantern, as it were—by dressing up in a modified gorilla suit and entertaining guests at the local Moose Club.

It is a calling she takes very seriously. Her late husband, Billy, wrote a ballad about the Bardin Booger called, appropriately enough, "The Bardin Booger." Lena followed up with her own composition, "The Bardin Booger's Christmas Wish," which is musically significant in two ways: (1) we learn the Booger wants a wife for Christmas, and (2) it is the only known recording that attempts to rhyme the words "brief" and "wish."

★ ★

"I think there's something out there," said Lena Crain. "I'm just not sure what. A circus came to this area some years back. Maybe a gorilla escaped and mated with something."

Lena's Booger costume is a reflection of that suspicion. It's basically a gorilla suit onto which she sewed a pair of ears. She also painted the lips red and the teeth white, just to jazz it up a bit. She takes her act to service club meetings, schools, festivals—wherever the services of a Booger are needed. Unlike her woodsy counterpart, Lena is a gentle, people-friendly kind of Booger who takes great pains not to frighten children.

"The little ones get scared if you growl or jump around too much," she explains.

Her act is usually accompanied by Billy's song, the chorus of which goes like this:

Hey, Mr. Bardin Booger!
Bardin is your home.
And every day you love to roam.
You run through the bushes and you run through the trees.
Hey, Mr. Bardin Booger,
Don't you get me, please!

Besides inspiring a couple of songs, the prospect of an odiferous half-gorilla, half-something roaming the piney woods of northeast Florida proved to be a crude but effective disciplinary tool.

"Parents had no trouble keeping their kids close to home," Lena said. "They told them if they strayed too far, the Booger would get them."

Meanwhile, back at Bud's Grocery, which, by the way, carries stovepipes if you happen to need one, we asked clerk Norma Key if she had any personal knowledge of the Bardin Booger.

"I sure do," she said. "I married him."

If you need a Bardin Booger for a local function, Lena Crain can be reached at (386) 328-6665. She says she has updated her Booger mask, the details of which we cannot divulge on pain of something hairy and stinky appearing on our front porch.

A *Florida Curiosities* exclusive! A never-before-published,
unretouched photograph of the reclusive Bardin Booger.
Look hard and you can see Elvis at the far end of the tracks.

We Ain't Afraid of No Ghosts
Cassadaga

There is no truth to the rumor that there is a closet full of ectoplasm inside Cassadaga's Colby Memorial Temple.

And even if there were, the stuff would not be the greenish slime of *Ghostbusters* fame, but rather "gray and smoky, with the feel of cobwebs," according to the Rev. Jim Watson, an ordained Cassadaga Spiritualist minister who claims to have seen the stuff.

Located between Orlando and Daytona Beach, the tiny village of Cassadaga bills itself as the Psychic Center of the World and, more defensibly, the Oldest Spiritualist Center in the South. Now the home of around one hundred more-or-less permanent residents, Cassadaga was founded in 1894 by George P. Colby, a New York Spiritualist who was told by a medium that he would one day establish a Spiritualist community in the South. According to legend, Colby followed his Indian spirit guide, Seneca, through the Florida wilderness until he came to the precise spot he had seen in his séance, which today is on the outskirts of Deltona, within whiffing distance of the exhaust fumes of Interstate 4.

The Cassadaga Spiritualist Camp, situated on fifty-seven acres of rolling woodland, is a tightly knit community of Spiritualists, mediums, psychics, and healers. (If you're looking for fortune-tellers, tarot card readers, and crystal ball gazers, their shops are on the other side of the street.)

Spiritualists believe in continuous life and connection with the spiritual world. Needless to say, the camp is a popular place to visit at Halloween, and lots of ghost stories are based in Cassadaga.

But during daylight hours Cassadaga is a quaint, non-ghostly assemblage of lovely late-nineteenth- and early-twentieth-century homes. It was added to the National Register of Historic Places in 1991. The Cassadaga Hotel—built in 1901, destroyed by fire in 1925, and rebuilt in 1927—is a charming building with rockers spaced about its wraparound porch. After a haircut and lunch at the hotel,

★ ★

you can wander across the street to the Spiritualist Camp for a psychic reading or a regression into a past life.

Just watch out for the ectoplasm.

For more information call (386) 228-3171 or pay an online visit to www.cassadaga.org/.

Marjorie Kinnan Rawlings and *The Yearling*
Cross Creek

A tour of the Marjorie Kinnan Rawlings Historic State Park begins with a marker and excerpt from *Cross Creek,* her 1942 novel: "It is necessary to leave the impersonal highway, to step inside the rusty gate

Fruit-bearing citrus trees fill the front yard of the Marjorie Kinnan Rawlings home in Cross Creek, Florida.

★ ★

and leave it behind. One is now inside the orange grove, out of one world and in the mysterious heart of another. And after long years of spiritual homelessness, of nostalgia, here is that mystic loveliness of childhood again. Here is home."

The fact that this placard stands in an orange grove, just inside a rusty gate, is letter perfect.

For literary fans of *Cross Creek* and *The Yearling,* the latter made into a movie with Gregory Peck, the Rawlings site covers familiar ground. She wrote about her farm house, citrus groves, and nearby Orange Lake, and here they all are. On the broad, screened veranda where Rawlings served meals, an orange tabby cat surveys visitors with sleepy eyes.

Rawlings moved to the seventy-two-acre farm in 1928, after a spring vacation in Florida. She began writing and won the Pulitzer Prize in 1938 for *The Yearling,* the story of a young boy and his fawn coming of age.

She later wrote *Cross Creek* and then *Cross Creek Cookery,* as someone confident of her culinary capabilities. "For my part, my literary ability may safely be questioned as harshly as one wills," Rawlings wrote, "but indifference to my table puts me into a rage."

The Marjorie Kinnan Rawlings Historic State Park is southeast of Gainesville on County Road 325 in Cross Creek. Admission is charged. To contact the park, dial (352) 466-3672.

Changing Flats for Fun?
Daytona Beach

After a long drive to Florida, most tourists have had enough of roads and traffic, lines and delays, noise and fumes. Car sickness, to one degree or another, is common. The very idea of having to change a flat tire, in a hurry and with crowds watching, is enough to send them over the edge.

At the Daytona 500 Experience, people pay for the privilege.

The motor-sports attraction offers NASCAR exhibits, motion

The Perils of Pronunciation

Generations of Orlando tourists have puzzled over the pronunciation of Kissimmee, a city southeast of Disney World. The great temptation is to pronounce it *kissy-me,* but locals give it a broad Southern twang: *kuh-sim-ee.*

In Miami, which has become a modern Babel of languages and ethnicities, you hardly ever hear the pronunciation of the city given by early residents. Just about everyone ends the word with an *ee,* these days, but some old-timers still call it *mi-am-uh.*

Lake Okeechobee, the shallow heart of south Florida, is pronounced with a *ka* rather than a *kee.* Like this: *oh-ka-cho-bee.*

North of Miami, there is Boca Raton, which is not pronounced like a rodent. It's *ruh-tone.* The first word in Hobe Sound is pronounced *ho-bee.* Near Melbourne on the Space Coast is the small town of Eau Gallie, which begins with the French word for water. It ends up being less like *oh, golly* and more like *oh, galley.*

In the Florida Keys, Islamorada gets the appropriate Spanish pronunciation: *eye-la-mor-ah-da.* So does Bahia Honda, which usually gets slurred into something like *bay-uh hon-da.* West of Key West is Dry Tortugas National Park. The name comes from the Spanish word from turtle: *tor-too-guhs.*

On the south Gulf Coast, there is a lovely island called Captiva. The place is captivating, but it's called *cap-tee-va.* There is also a little community called El Jobean. It's not Spanish, though; developer Joel Bean had a sense of humor.

North of Tampa, a long-running mermaid show has drawn thousands of tourists to Weeki Wachee. Locals call it *wick-ee watch-ee.*

South of Gainesville is an antiques center called Micanopy, but visitors must fight the temptation of *my canopy.* It's more like *mick-uh-no-pee.*

In Tampa, the historic cigar-rolling center is Ybor City. It doesn't sound like *Why,* though. It's *ee-bore* city. To the east, there's a small town called Wimauma. Newcomers often try to mumble an unaccented *wi-maw-ma.* Locals, though, give a strong emphasis to the first syllable: *why-momma.*

Panhandle visitors often pause at DeFuniak Springs. The name is no "fun," though. It's more like *de-foon-ee-ack* springs.

simulators, and tours of the world-famous Daytona International Speedway. Then there's the Ford 16-Second Pit Stop Challenge, in which visitors race to change a race car tire. Never have so many people enjoyed handling a car jack, power drill, and oversize tire.

As of yet, the Daytona 500 Experience doesn't have any blown radiator challenges or fiery collision simulators.

What it does have are museum displays that trace the history of racing on Daytona Beach, where the firm-packed sand first drew cars in the early 1900s. Later on, Bill France, the founder of NASCAR, designed a beach race course and charged admission. To discourage gate crashers, he posted signs that read BEWARE OF RATTLESNAKES.

Now that NASCAR has become such a huge success, filling 150,000-seat stadiums, attendance is not a problem. The Daytona 500 Experience puts the bite on enthusiastic fans by charging extra for the Dream Laps and Acceleration Alley simulator games. The Pit Stop Challenge, though, is still included in the general admission price.

Apparently, charging people extra to change tires would be asking too much.

The Daytona 500 Experience is at 1801 West International Speedway Boulevard. Admission is $24.99 for adults and $19.99 for children six to twelve. Children under six get in free. Hours are 10:00 a.m. to 7:00 p.m. every day except Christmas, with extended hours during peak times. For more information, call (386) 681-6800.

Florida's World-Famous Bike Week
Daytona Beach

Each year, thousands of motorcyclists roar into Daytona Beach for Bike Week, a celebration that is half reunion, half trade show, and half Mardi Gras. If this adds up to more than a whole, well, that's the general idea. The annual motorcycle extravaganza offers races and rallies, parties and concerts, smoke shops and strip shows, but everything begins with the daily parade of bikes down Main Street, where the traffic signs read motorcycles only.

★ ★

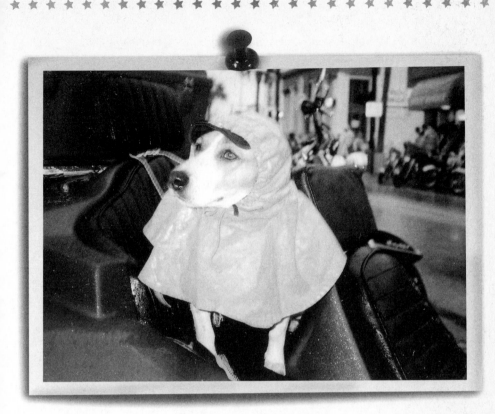

Even the dogs like to look sharp during Bike Week.

If you haven't cruised the strip, then you haven't been to Bike Week.

When a Harley-Davidson kicks to a start, with an open throttle and fat pipes, you can feel it in your boots. When one hundred Harleys rumble from a curb, and the leather chaps crowd cheers at the corner of Main Street and Atlantic Avenue, you can feel it in your bones. This is the sight, sound, and overwhelming sensation of Bike Week.

There are lots of bikers at Bike Week. More bikers than you've ever seen before. More than you'll ever see anywhere else. Fat bikers and skinny bikers. Old bikers and young bikers. Bald bikers, bikers with hair, and bikers with ponytails. Bikers on laid-back choppers, and bikers on forward-leaning racers. Bikers with babes, bikers with kids, bikers with kids in sidecars.

There are bikers who look like Neil Young. Bikers who look like Vince Neil. Bikers who look like Neil Sedaka.

There seems to be lots of drinking on Daytona Beach, and some ladies flashing and men hollering, but old-timers agree that Bike Week ain't so bad these days. Tourism might be the great equalizer. Even the burliest biker doesn't look so tough toting a bright shopping bag from Yukon Jack's Custom Leather. Even the toughest tough guy looks a little silly taking out a disposable camera for a souvenir snapshot. Lots of bikers bring their families these days, and some bike-watchers roll babies in strollers.

During one recent Bike Week, on a crowded corner of Main Street, surrounded by grizzled guys in Harley black, two young flutists played quietly for tips. A sign explained that the local girls were raising money for a band trip to France. A block down the street, Ed Zima of South Daytona Beach posed for photos with his dog Spike, a beagle. What makes Ed and Spike such an attraction? Well, both the dog and owner wear matching leather vests and caps.

Bike Week is held in late February or early March each year. For details phone (386) 255-0981 or log on to www.daytonachamber.com.

The Skydiving Guru of DeLand
DeLand

If skydiving has a world capital, it's DeLand, Florida, a small university town north of Orlando. SkyDive DeLand is a leading drop zone, and *Skydiving* magazine is published just a few blocks from the municipal airport. There are two harness makers nearby, along with the world's largest maker of parachute canopies. There's also Bill Booth, the free thinker who patented modern chute rigging and revolutionized the sport with tandem skydiving.

Booth is a Miami native who wears a ZZ Top beard and lives in a pyramid-shaped house on a lake just outside of town. Although he graduated from the University of Florida with a degree in music education, of all things, he also had an engineering background, along with a passion for skydiving and perfect timing.

The man who revolutionized skydiving is also the hands-down winner of the ZZ Top look-alike contest.

★ ★

"When I started jumping in 1965, the gear was basically unchanged from 1918, so I came along at the right time," he says. "I'm not an engineer type; I'm an inventor type. I think differently than other people, apparently."

Booth taught skydiving before developing the rigging that is found on virtually all modern parachutes. He also helped come up with the idea of tandem rigging that would allow an instructor to accompany a student to the ground. There was only one way to test the idea.

"I took my secretary and just went up and did it," he says.

After delicate negotiations with the Federal Aeronautics Administration (he'd broken regulations by making these development flights), he got approval for tandem skydiving. It's revolutionized the sport, giving beginners a chance for the full skydiving experience. Along the way, Booth became something of a celebrity.

"When I made *National Geographic,* my mom was impressed," he boasts. "When I made MTV, my kids were impressed."

Tom Cruise took skydiving lessons while filming *Days of Thunder* in nearby Daytona Beach. He got to know Booth and later got him a bit part in *The Firm.* One of Booth's favorite stories is about another skydiving student asking him to sign his log book after a training jump.

"This kid comes up with a pen, walks right past Tom Cruise, and says, 'Are you Bill Booth?'" he says, laughing. "And Cruise's jaw just dropped. I said, 'I bet that never happened to you before.' So for once in my life I upstaged Tom Cruise."

Today Booth continues to run his company, Relative Workshop, which he's renamed The Uninsured Relative Workshop to help reduce liability. He's known throughout the skydiving world for both tandem jumps and his trademark beard. That personal touch dates back to his days as a close-cropped schoolteacher.

"I always said if I had my own company, I'd never shave again," he says. "Now I'm like Colonel Sanders, and I'm stinking stuck with it."

✦ ✦

The Flip-Your-Own-Pancake Restaurant
DeLeon Springs

Seven miles north of DeLand, within the DeLeon Springs State Recreation Area, is the Old Spanish Sugar Mill Grill and Griddle House.
Moss-draped oaks line the road to the restaurant, and the front door
is just a few feet from the crystal-clear water of the natural spring.
The Sugar Mill Grill starts serving breakfast at 9:00 a.m. on weekdays,
8:00 a.m. on the weekends, and lots of people will wait an hour or
two in line for a table.

The secret to this success? There's an electric griddle in the center
of each table where you cook your own pancakes, eggs, and French
toast. Waitresses bring out all the ingredients, including flour ground
on French buhrstones, and the whole thing is homey and fun. Patricia
Schwarze, who took over the place from her father, doesn't know of
any other restaurant like it.

"It's a lot of work, an astounding amount of work, considering
that people cook their own food," she says, laughing. "But you need
extra staff and, from a restaurant point of view, the tables turn over
really slowly. It's insane, quite frankly, but we have a lot of fun with
it. It's the play interaction that makes it work. We give people batter
and let them play."

Patricia's father, a fifth-generation gristmiller, had a New York
bakery in the 1920s. He'd set a griddle on the counter, and it would
become a convivial meeting place for local customers. Years later,
Schwarze brought the idea to Florida, after restoring the old mill at
DeLeon Springs in 1961.

"He was a character, quite the raconteur," Patricia says. "Those
are my early memories, of sitting around here with the storytellers."

The Sugar Mill Grill remains a distinctive place. A huge mill wheel
dominates one side of the restaurant, and there's a brick fireplace
along another wall. Payment is on something like an honor system.
On the way out, you tell the cashier what you had, and she rings it up
on the cash register.

★ ★

If cooking customers get a little too boisterous or messy, there's a waitress who jokes that they'll be washing their dishes, too.

DeLeon Springs State Recreation Area is 7 miles north of DeLand on State Road 17. The Old Spanish Sugar Mill Grill and Griddle House is open from 9:00 a.m. to 5:00 p.m. on weekdays, 8:00 a.m. to 5:00 p.m. on weekends. Expect a long wait in line in winter and on weekends. You can reach the restaurant at (386) 985–5644.

Eight Flags over Amelia Island
Fernandina Beach

You've heard of Six Flags Over Texas? Forget that. Florida's Amelia Island, north of Jacksonville, has a checkered history that requires unflagging attention. No fewer than eight banners have flown over the island.

First there were the French. Jean Ribault named the place Isle de Mai after landing on May 3, 1562. Next came the Spanish, who defeated the French and founded St. Augustine down the coast. They named the island Santa Maria after a mission there.

That mission was destroyed in 1702 by the English, who named the island Amelia in honor of the daughter of George II. Following the Revolutionary War, Britain ceded Florida back to Spain. Thomas Jefferson's Embargo Act closed U.S. ports to shipping, and Fernandina Beach became infamous for smugglers and pirates.

With U.S. backing, the "Patriots of Amelia Island" overthrew the Spanish in 1812 and raised their own flag, replacing it with the Stars and Stripes the next day. Spain demanded the island back and built Fort San Carlos, only to see it seized by Sir Gregor MacGregor, who raised the Green Cross of Florida flag over the fort in 1817. He withdrew, but later that year another uprising brought the Mexican Rebel flag to the island.

Finally, in 1821, Spain ceded Amelia Island to the United States, which built Fort Clinch on the north shore. Confederate forces took the fort briefly during the Civil War, but Union troops regained the island in 1862. It's been part of the United States ever since, through boom and bust, pulp mills and shrimp fleets, and now boasts of luxury resorts such as the Ritz-Carlton and Amelia Island Plantation.

For those keeping score at home, Amelia Island history goes something like this: French, Spanish, English, Spanish, Patriots, Green Cross of Florida, Mexican Rebel, United States, Confederate States, United States.

Climbing "Mount Gator"
Gainesville

For the last decade, at least, the most famous gators in the state have played football for the University of Florida. The Gators won national championships in 2006 and 2008. Quarterback Tim Tebow became a folk hero, Florida's answer to Paul Bunyan, with a fame that inspired jokes about his extraordinary abilities.

"Tim Tebow counted to infinity—twice." "Superman wears Tim

University of Florida students enjoy spirited workouts at Florida Field.

★ ★

Tebow pajamas." "When Google can't find something, it asks Tim Tebow for help."

College football fans make pilgrimages to Gainesville, home of Florida Field at Ben Hill Griffin Stadium. Many visitors take pictures beside the long, low statue of "Bull Gator." Some who wander around the stadium are surprised to find that it is open to the public most days from 7 a.m. to 10 p.m.

Spokesmen for the UF athletic department don't know if this practice is unique, but they do know that most universities lock their stadiums to keep people out. In Gainesville, fans aren't allowed on the field, but they can walk around and take pictures at the "Home of the Gators."

Lots of students run laps around the stadium or jog up and down the steps. The east side of the huge arena features an unbroken climb of ninety steps. This is known as "Mount Gator"—a serious workout.

"I usually do a snake, going up one side of steps and down another," says David Hutzel, a former student. "It's more exciting than running on a treadmill."

Bogeys under the Lights
Gainesville

It's not necessary to travel to Alaska if you want to play golf at midnight. The opportunity is available at Gainesville's West End Golf Club, advertised as the "World's Largest Lighted Golf Course."

How do they know this to be true? "*Golf Digest* did an article saying we were the largest lighted golf course in the world and nobody disputed it," said club employee Stan Mitchell.

So there you have it.

Open since 1968, West End is 3,940 yards long and plays to a par of sixty. There are six par fours, the longest a formidable 430-yarder, and twelve par threes ranging from 135 yards to 188 yards. The course record is 53, shot by head pro Scott Dombek.

You can play the course by day, if you wish, but to get the true

★ ★

West End experience, you have to tee it up after the sun goes down. The lights give the terrain an eerie quality and also cast some distracting shadows. The tees and greens are well-lighted, but there are some dark spots if you veer too far from the fairway on the longer holes.

The word at West End is, if you're going to slice it, slice it next to one of the light poles. You get a free drop if they impede your swing.

Besides being relatively cheap, West End is also a great way to beat the summer heat. Just remember to pay attention to the golfers around you. Golf balls hurt just as much at night as they do during the day.

The West End Golf Club is located 3½ miles west of Interstate 75 on State Road 26. The course is open from 7:00 a.m. to midnight. During the winter months, the course is closed at night on weekends. Call (352) 332–2721 or visit www.westendgolf.com.

Gators Love Their Burrito Brothers

Gainesville

For University of Florida alumni, there's nothing like returning to campus for a Saturday night football game. It's a chance to wear orange and blue, sing "We Are the Boys of Old Florida," and eat at Burrito Brothers, a Gainesville institution for decades. On some nights, the wait in line—for takeout, mind you—can be more than an hour.

For Gators who can't make it to Gainesville, the restaurant ships frozen burritos as far as California and Hawaii.

"We do a lot of orders for Gator Clubs around the Southeast," says Randy Akerson, who founded the restaurant with his wife, Janet. "We send a huge order to Chicago every year. It's mind-boggling."

Janet's a former English major; Randy dropped out of the UF law school after injuring his back. While working at a nearby sub shop, he got an offer to start a little Mexican restaurant just across the street from campus. The place took its name from a 1970s country-rock group, the Flying Burrito Brothers.

(Continued on page 52)

Truly Nolen's Mouse Mobiles

Florida residents learn to take them for granted, like sunshine and fresh orange juice, but the bright yellow vehicles draw stares from newcomers and tourists. Once the color catches their eyes, the whimsical mouse ears and tail usually draw a smile or two. How often do you see a mouse mobile rolling down the highway?

The fact that these vehicles advertise a pest control company takes some explaining.

Truly Nolen, the son of a Miami exterminator, graduated from the University of Florida with a degree in entomology. He moved to Tucson, Arizona, in 1955 to start his own bug business. When his wife's car broke down, he painted his name and number on the side as a garage billboard of sorts. People responded, so he bought another car, and then another one.

By 1961 Nolen had expanded to Florida, tried painting a truck red to represent a fire ant, and then decided on bright yellow Volkswagen Beetles with black ears, whiskers, and tails.

The rest is pest control advertising history.

Today Truly Nolen is the third largest exterminating company in the country, and mouse mobiles roll across most of Arizona and Florida. The cars are accompanied by silly catchphrases such as "Adios, cucaracha" and "Nite-nite, termite." An employee coined the latest slogan, "Ears and tails above the rest," to win a company contest.

Truly Nolen is an unusual name to begin with, and the mice make it even more memorable.

"It's a great icebreaker," says Barry Murray, director of company public relations in Hollywood, Florida. "Some of our drivers get scared, because people will jump out at a red light and start snapping pictures. Some of our single sales guys say it's a chick magnet, too."

The cars have also drawn attention at the other Hollywood, the one in California. In the 2000 Burt Reynolds movie *The Crew*, hapless bank robbers use a mouse mobile to pull off a heist.

"We've been in about six movies, and we've never paid to be in one," Murray says. "They call us. Everyone knows our humorous edge."

Truly Nolen's mouse mobiles have

evolved and improved over the years. The metal ears used to slow the cars down, because they blocked so much wind, so an employee came up with the idea of hinges that allow them to lay back at speeds greater than 25 miles per hour. Today the mice are the second most recognized advertising vehicle in the country, after the Oscar Meyer Wienermobile.

Among children, the Truly Nolen vehicles are especially popular.

"We're the only pest control company that gets called for car day at schools, along with the fire trucks and everything," Murray says. "That's always dangerous, though, because we know we'll have a broken tail by the end of the day. So we always bring an extra one."

★ ★

(Continued from page 49)

"When I started in Gainesville, there were only two or three Mexican restaurants, including the large chain I won't name," Randy says. "Now there's much more traffic and much more competition. We haven't changed, though, and that gives us a little romantic cachet."

Black bean and pinto bean burritos and tacos are on the menu, along with fresh homemade salsa and guacamole. Nothing fancy, nothing expensive. The place has never expanded, never franchised, and never lost the hole-in-the-wall charm that made it a success in the first place.

When the original home of Burrito Brothers was sold and demolished a few years ago, the restaurant moved a few hundred feet down University Avenue. The new space behind the Presbyterian Student Center offers patio seating.

The Burrito Brothers Taco Co. is at 1402 West University Avenue. For more information call (352) 378-5948.

The Mystique of Devil's Millhopper
Gainesville

Devil's Millhopper, Gainesville's giant sinkhole and state geological site, got its fearsome name from Florida settlers in the nineteenth century. They compared the shape of the hole to the funnel of a gristmill that fed flour into a grinder. Only this earthen mill apparently fed bodies to the devil. Why else would there be fossilized bones and teeth at the bottom?

Pretty good PR for what amounts to a hole in the ground, 120 feet deep and 500 feet across.

Devil's Millhopper became a destination for early Florida train travelers, with picture postcards of the site dating back to 1906. Erosion took its toll before the state bought the sixty-two-acre site in 1974. Park workers built a wooden staircase to help prevent erosion and maintain a lush landscape nourished by spring-fed waterfalls.

What captured the imagination of early settlers now soothes the souls of late-afternoon visitors.

★ ★

Devil's Millhopper Geological State Park is at 4732 Millhopper Road, Gainesville. Hours are 9:00 a.m. to 5:00 p.m. Wednesday through Sunday. Closed Monday and Tuesday. Admission is charged; call (352) 955-2008.

"The First Hollywood"
Jacksonville

If visitors to Jacksonville wander through the city's historic neighborhoods, they might stumble across a sign for "Norman Studios" on Arlington Road. The abandoned buildings there are all that's left of a silent film industry that went boom and bust before the world had ever heard of Hollywood.

In his 2009 book, *The First Hollywood,* Shawn Bean describes the silent film history of North Florida, along with tantalizing ideas of what might have been.

"To talk about Jacksonville is to talk about Metro-Goldwyn-Mayer (MGM), Fox Broadcasting Company, Oliver Hardy, D. W. Griffith, Mary Pickford, the Barrymore family, and the advent of Technicolor. Approximately 300 films were produced in Jacksonville from 1909 to 1926. This was no one-off pit stop. The city was THIS CLOSE to becoming the country's premiere destination for movie production. It's not that hard to imagine."

Moviemakers from New York City traveled by train to Jacksonville for the winter sunshine, especially, along with the Florida landscape and Southern setting. The first film made in Jacksonville was *A Florida Feud; Or, Love in the Everglades.* Another early movie was called *The Cracker's Bride.*

The most bizarre Jacksonville movie might have been *A Florida Enchantment,* from 1914, which featured two actresses in blackface and cross-dressing roles. The plot follows a woman and her servant after they swallow magical sex-change seeds from Africa. Many years later, this "proto-gay" film was discussed in popular books such as *The Celluloid Closet* and academic studies such as *Queering the Color*

Line: Race and the Invention of Homosexuality in American Culture.

Norman Studios, founded by a white businessman named Richard Norman, made films featuring black actors for black audiences. Its first movie, *Sleepy Sam the Sleuth,* was a comedy featuring a bumbling detective. Bill Pickett, a black rodeo cowboy, starred in films such as *The Bull-Dogger* and *The Crimson Skull.*

By the 1920s, Hollywood's star had eclipsed Jacksonville's. World War I made the city a busy port, less dependent on early film studios. The winner of the 1917 mayoral election campaigned against the moviemakers from out of town. A flu epidemic and business slump also drove out producers. North Florida filmmaking simply faded away.

Outside of Jacksonville, this early chapter in American cinema is hardly known. Local groups are still raising money for the Norman Studios Silent Film Museum at 6335 Arlington Road.

For more information, visit NormanStudios.org.

The King Slept Here
Jacksonville

Maybe the heat and humidity reminded him of his home in Tupelo, Mississippi, but for whatever reason, Elvis Presley loved performing in Florida.

Between 1955 and 1977, the year he died, the King did seventeen shows in Jacksonville alone. One of his movies, *Follow That Dream,* was filmed in several north-central Florida locations. Interior scenes were shot in an Ocala bank building and in the Inverness courthouse.

It was at the August 10, 1956, show at Jacksonville's Florida Theater that Elvis's "controversial" pelvis gyrations first made national headlines. Juvenile court judge Marion Gooding attended the concert to see what all the fuss was about. The judge did not become an instant fan; in fact, he came away convinced that Elvis was undermining the youth of America and told Elvis if he wiggled his hips during the second show, he would have him arrested.

Miffed, but respectful of authority, Elvis made no movements during his second show except to wave his pinkie. The crowd, needless to say, loved it.

When doing shows in Jacksonville between 1972 and 1977, Elvis always stayed at the Hilton (now the Crowne Plaza Jacksonville Riverfront). After he left his room in the morning, hotel maids would cut up his bed sheets into 2-inch squares and sell them to the throngs of fans gathered outside. If you're planning on staying at the hotel and want to feel like the King for a night, ask for room 1010, otherwise known as the Elvis Room.

To reserve a room, call the Crowne Plaza at (904) 398-8800.

Dealing with People Who Cross the Line
Jennings

Tourists who cross from Georgia into Florida on I-75 may believe that they will immediately encounter an alligator, Mickey Mouse, or a swarm of mosquitoes. Instead, they are greeted by Patrick Burke, the manager of one of five visitor welcome centers strung along Florida's northern boundary. His employees have sixty years of combined experience handing out complimentary cups of Florida orange juice and answering tourists' questions that range from "How far to Disney World?" (214 miles) to "Are alligators dangerous?" (yes, especially if you feed them) or "Where's the nearest nudist camp?" (the staff keeps a file).

The offer of free orange or grapefruit juice, maps, and information draws 2.5 million visitors a year to the state's five welcome centers. At the center on I-75, just north of Jennings, the staff pours 1,500 gallons of juice a month, four ounces at a time. Unlike earlier days, you can have more than one serving.

To work at a Florida visitor center, you have to pass a hundred-question test dealing with Florida government, history, and tourist attractions, both major and minor. Besides Disney World, tourists also ask where they can find a mock-up of the Hanoi Hilton (Pensacola),

★ ★

where they can drive a real Winston Cup race car (Orlando), and how the town of Two Egg got its name (residents bartered eggs for other goods; two eggs was the minimum for a trade).

Probably the most frequently asked question is whether the visitor center gives away free or reduced-price tickets to Disney World. (No. You have to stop at one of the Disney-affiliated tourist centers farther down the road for these.) Occasionally, there is a mini crisis to deal with. More often than you would like to think, visitors leave kids or pets behind. Although these oversights are usually noticed fairly quickly, there have been times when a husband towing a mobile home has driven away, not realizing that his wife has gotten out of

Folks who stop at the Florida Welcome Center just north of Jennings on I-75 can get a free cup of orange juice and directions to the nearest nudist camp.

★ ★

the vehicle to go to the restroom. Sometimes it's hours before the husband realizes anything is amiss.

The visitor welcome center on I-75 is such a popular place that it actually became a roadside hazard. The state had to move the welcome to Florida sign back off the highway because tourists were getting out of their cars and posing to have their pictures taken. With cars and trucks whipping by at 70-plus miles per hour, there was understandable concern that someone would get killed.

But today, the visitor center is just a friendly place to stop, have a cup of juice, and maybe ask directions.

"Is this a fresh map?" an elderly lady in sunglasses asks. "Yes, ma'am," answers employee Patricia Brown, trying not to roll her eyes. "It's the freshest one we've got."

Antiquing Mecca
Mount Dora

Mount Dora has scenic canoe trails and quaint bed-and-breakfasts, but what the town is really famous for is its antiques.

No, we're not talking about the citizenry; we're talking about a huge concentration of vendors selling everything from old iron gates to ceramic roosters.

Located about a half-hour's drive north of Orlando, Mount Dora is the antiques capital of Florida. You can spend hours, if not days, checking out the seemingly endless array of stores and stalls. The action gets really heavy several times a year when Renninger's antiques stages weekend extravaganzas that attract throngs of people and around 1,000 dealers. For dates and admission prices check out www.renningers.com.

If you want to avoid the crowds, choose a day when Renninger's is not hosting one of its big shows. You'll still find plenty of old stuff that you never knew you needed.

Mount Dora has an elevation of 184 feet above sea level, which by Florida standards qualifies it as a mountain town. Some homes even

have basements, which in this part of the country are about as rare
as snowstorms. Once you get over your altitude sickness (just kidding), you can stroll the quaint streets of this town of 11,000 souls
and visit the many gift shops, fashion boutiques, cafes and art galleries. Or you can simply find a comfortable place to sit and admire Lake
Dora below, one of 1,400 named lakes in Lake County. If you want
to know more about the Keyhole Vortex (and who doesn't?), sign
up for the Mount Dora Ghost Walk. It's a rather convoluted ninety-
minute panache of history, legend and myth compiled by a group
of volunteer historians and local actors. (Caution: If you're afraid of
marionettes, this tour may not be for you.) If you want to impress
your friends and/or relatives, tell them that Mount Dora was the site
of the 1981 film *Honkey Tonk Freeway.* Many buildings were painted
pink as part of the set and an Indian elephant was shipped in and
taught to water ski on Lake Dora. (We're sorry we missed that.) History buffs will want to visit the Lakeside Inn at 100 North Alexander
Street. The wooden building dates back to 1883 and has lodged such
notables as Calvin Coolidge, Thomas Edison, Henry Ford, and Dwight
D. Eisenhower. Mount Dora provides a nice break from the madhouse
of Disney World and other Orlando attractions. When you get tired of
antiquing, you can go fishing in Lake Dora or simply chill out with a
glass of wine at one of the many cafes. As for us, we're still looking
for the perfect ceramic rooster. For more information, visit www
.mountdora.com.

A Land Bridge across I-75
Ocala

From I-75, it looks like any other overpass in Florida. From the seat of
a bike or a horse, though, the Cross Florida Greenway land bridge is
something else: a trail link, the shape of things to come, and a defiant
step against the tyranny of interstate traffic.

Local advocates call the land bridge the first of its kind in the
United States. The $3.4 million overpass is 52 feet wide and 200 feet

long, following a natural ridge across the interstate about 9 miles
south of Ocala. The specially designed supports carry fieldstone walls,
tons of topsoil, and irrigated planters with oaks, pines, and native
vegetation.

"This bridge is the bridge of the twenty-first century," said David
Struhs, secretary for the Department of Environmental Protection
(DEP), at the 2000 grand opening. "It will connect 15 miles of biking trails, 56 miles of equestrian trails, and 40 miles of hiking trails,
but this bridge will also reconnect Floridians back to the land and will
connect us to our new future."

The land bridge also allows small animals—foxes, raccoons, and
possums—to cross what had been a busy barrier of traffic along I-75.
As of yet, local animals haven't left any signs, but it's easy to imagine
wildlife graffiti: "I brake for bipeds." "My cub is an honor student
in the Ocala National Forest." "If this tree is a-rockin', don't come
a-knockin'."

Back in the real world, the land bridge has managed to bring
together hikers, bikers, and horsemen, groups traditionally at odds
with one another. Kenneth Smith, the local section head for the Florida Trail Association, was presented with a DEP plaque honoring that
cooperation.

"We can't stop the interstates; they're part of our lives," he said.
"But we can't let them stop us, either."

The Ocala land bridge crosses I-75 north, north of exit 67. The
nearest trailhead is east of the interstate on County Road 475A in
Belleview. For more information call the Office of Greenways and
Trails at (352) 236-7143.

What a Drag
Ocala

At the "Big Daddy" Don Garlits Museum of Drag Racing, you might
actually run into the "Swamp Rat" himself. The seventy-eight-year-old
legend and his wife, Pat, live in a house on the grounds, and it's not

★ ★

unusual for him to stop by the museum, chat with visitors, and maybe share a story or two about what it was like to cover a quarter mile in 4.72 seconds at a top speed of 303.27 miles per hour.

Garlits is clear on the details because he did it at the age of sixty-nine at the Indianapolis Speedway. It was his own personal lifetime speed record, which is pretty remarkable for a man who has been racing cars for more than half a century and has won just about every trophy and award the sport can bestow.

While other men his age contemplate their next nap or a few vigorous hands of bridge, Garlits continues to tinker with dragsters, occasionally racing them. He does this despite suffering near-fatal burns in a 1959 accident in Chester, South Carolina, and losing half his right foot when a transmission exploded in 1969.

Garlits, by the way, was given his nickname by his daughters, who used to watch him from the stands while shouting, "Go, daddy! Go, daddy! Go, daddy!" A track announcer modified the chant and began calling him Big Daddy, which is a bit of a joke because he stands no taller than five-nine.

The museum, which Garlits opened in 1983, contains about 150 drag racers with names like *Pandemonium, Pollutionizer, Bounty Hunter,* and *Yellow Fang.* Garlits's cars, painted in trademark black, include *Swamp Rat 22,* the famous dragster that set the 1975 world speed record (250.69 miles per hour in 5.63 seconds) that stood for seven years. Nearby is *Swamp Rat 27,* a 1981 model that was powered by a supercharged, fuel-injected, 454-cubic-inch Dodge Hemi engine that generated 2,700 horsepower and could cover the quarter-mile track in 6.20 seconds at a top speed of 230 miles per hour. The car burned "nitro," which is short for nitromethane. You never hear drag racers complain about the price of unleaded regular; a gallon of nitro goes for $40.

Garlits is credited with many innovations in drag racing, including the rear-mounted engine, bicycle tires on the front, and driver canopies. Called the King of the Dragsters, Garlits set numerous speed records and has won 144 national events and 17 world titles.

At the museum, it's rather odd to see all that power sitting in front of you, not moving. Drag racing is all about flames and smoking tires and ear-splitting noise. The cars on display here are as quiet as extinct dinosaurs. But if you're a fan of drag racing, none of that will matter. The exhibits will bring back memories of great cars and the men who raced them.

For those who prefer slower, quieter vehicles, there is a Classic Car Collection next door to the drag racing museum. Cars from the early 1900s to the present are on display, including flathead Fords, a 1956 Chrysler sedan that once belonged to President Eisenhower, a 1950 Mercury that was once driven by "The Fonz" on the television show *Happy Days,* and a 1904 Orient Buckboard. Built mostly of wood, the Buckboard, at $375, was advertised as the "Cheapest Automobile in the World."

If you're not lucky enough to run into Big Daddy at his museum (we weren't), you can always sample his citrus. A box of grapefruits bearing a hand-lettered sign said they were from the Swamp Rat's own tree and were free for the taking.

The Museum of Drag Racing is located south of Ocala at 13700 S.W. 16th Avenue, just off I-75 exit 67. The museum and the Classic Car Collection are open daily from 9:00 a.m. to 5:00 p.m. Admission is charged. Call (352) 245-8661 or visit www.garlits.com.

Burgers, Shakes, and History, Too
Palatka

You know you're in a genuine Southern diner if the first question the waitress asks you when you plop down on a counter stool is, "Sweet tea, hon?"

Angels Diner, Florida's oldest, still does things pretty much the same way it's been doing them since it opened in 1932. You can

Angels Diner, Florida's oldest, occupies an old dining car in downtown Palatka. There's plenty of nostalgia, and the pusalows are to die for.

still order a pusalow—made with chocolate milk, vanilla syrup, and crushed ice—or a black bottom sandwich, which consists of bacon, scrambled eggs, and hamburger mixed together, grilled, and served on a bun.

Fashioned from an old railroad dining car, Angels has only ten counter stools and six tables, so the place fills up quickly. Overflow crowds can order curb service and sit at one of several picnic tables situated in the parking lot under a sheet metal overhang.

Angels, a local dining institution, is also popular with college kids headed off to St. Augustine Beach. Founded by Porter Angel and now owned by the Browning family, the diner is a must-stop for politicians campaigning in the area. Governor Jeb Bush had a bite to eat at Angels during his last campaign. (None of the waitresses could remember what he ordered, let alone what he said.)

A diner is nothing without nostalgia, and Angels has plenty, starting with the metal stairs leading up to the narrow door, passing by the trays on the wall urging you to drink Coca-Cola in bottles for 5 cents, and ending with the jukebox, where Fats Domino, the Andrews Sisters, and Elvis compete for airtime with Supertramp.

About the only concessions Angels has made to the passing of time are a no smoking sign next to the two tables by the door, and an air-conditioning system, the ductwork of which fits in nicely with the general diner decor.

More sweet tea, please, ma'am, and pass the ketchup.

Angels Diner is located at 209 Reid Street next to the Subway. It's open 6:00 a.m. to 9:00 p.m. Sunday through Thursday, and 6:00 a.m. to 10:00 p.m. Friday and Saturday. Phone (386) 325-3927.

Go, Fighting Sandcrabs!

Florida high schools have their share of Gators, Seminoles, and Hurricanes, following the traditions of state university athletic teams. There are also plenty of Lions, Tigers, and Bears—oh, my!—along with the usual Eagles, Wildcats, and Bulldogs.

Other schools are more creative, more original, when it comes to school mascots and nicknames.

Apopka High School features the Blue Darters, and at Admiral Farragut Academy in St. Petersburg, the players are Bluejackets, after the Union naval officer who stormed Mobile Bay during the Civil War.

Then there's the All Saints' Academy in Winter Haven. Yep, they're the Saints. The All Saints' Saints. The best players could form a team called The All Saints' All-Stars, or The All-Stars All Saints . . . something like that.

Nautical names float from the Gulf of Mexico to the Atlantic Ocean. There are the Charlotte High School Tarpons and the Coral Reef High School Barracudas. At Cocoa Beach High School, boys' and girls' teams are known simply as "The Beach." The Key West Conchs are named after a local seashell. Then there are the Lakeland Dreadnaughts, the Mariner Tritons, the Miami Beach Hi-Tides, the Miami Senior High Stingarees, and the Seabreeze High School Fighting Sandcrabs.

Father Lopez High School in Daytona Beach offers the Greenwaves. In Tallahassee, there are the Florida A&M Developmental School Baby Rattlers and Rattlerettes. Fort Lauderdale High School has the Flying L's. At Hialeah High School, near the famous racetrack, teams are the Thoroughbreds.

Then there are the Hilliard High School Flashes, the Howard Middle School Bumblebees and Lady Bumblebees, and the Laurel Hill High School Hoboes. Okeechobee High School offers the Brahmans. Osceola High has its Kowboys with a K. We have the Poplar Springs Atomics and the Tarpon Springs High School Spongers, after the local sponge-diving industry.

The Broward Christian School is diplomatic; they're the Ambassadors. Chiefland High School has the Indians—no surprise there. And Dixie M. Hollins High in St. Petersburg? The Rebels, of course.

Forest Capital of the South?

Perry

Florida's natural wonders include three national forests. The southern part of the state is dominated by Everglades National Forest, which is world famous for its unique ecosystem. In central Florida, there is Ocala National Forest, which offers a spectacular network of crystal-clear springs. Panhandle visitors often escape into Blackwater River National Forest.

Then there is Perry, Florida, billed as "Forest Capital of the South," with a state museum and everything. Of course, that museum is devoted to forestry, which is less about admiring trees than exploiting them. The pine trees of the region are grown as a crop to feed the

An 1864 cracker homestead shows how pioneers lived in Perry.

huge pulp mill that pollutes the Fenholloway River and gives Perry a sulfurous smell.

Sometimes, irony stinks.

The Forest Capital State Museum Park celebrates the importance of timber in the history of the state. Exhibits describe different native woods and their properties and uses. The longleaf pine, for instance, is used to create more than 5,000 products.

The best part of the park might be an 1864 cracker homestead which features antique furnishings and vintage farm equipment.

The thirteen-acre park is just south of Perry on US 19. Hours are 9 a.m. to noon and 1 to 5 p.m., Thursday through Monday, except for Thanksgiving, Christmas and New Year's. Each October, there is a Florida Forest Festival.

For more information, call (850) 584-3227.

That Sinking Feeling
Ponte Vedra Beach

If your idea of fun is watching your golf ball sink into a water hazard, then the 17th hole at the Tournament Players Club at Sawgrass is guaranteed to provide you one jolly good time.

Located in Ponte Vedra Beach, the TPC as it's known colloquially, is the home of the annual Players Championship. The best players in the world gather to compete in what some call golf's fifth major (the Masters, the U.S. Open, the British Open and the PGA being the original four major tournaments) and no hole gets the pros' attention more than the 17th.

A par-three that measures only 132 yards, the 17th—on paper at least—seems laughably easy. But the last laugh is usually on the golfer because the 17th's green is surrounded by water (not counting a narrow footpath leading to and from the green). It's a do-or-die tee shot: You either hit the green or your ball gets buried in a watery grave. Bob Tway made a 12 on the hole during the 2005 tournament by depositing four balls in the water (and then three-putting for good

**Pros and duffers alike have nightmares about the 17th
hole at the Tournament Players Club at Sawgrass.**
PHOTO COURTESY OF VISIT FLORIDA

measure). In the 2007 tournament, the pros hit fifty balls in the water
during the first round. All told that year, ninety-three balls made like
the *Titanic* and sank.

Golf fans are much like NASCAR fans in that they love wrecks. That
could explain why between 15,000 and 20,000 fans gather around the
tee of the 17th to watch the drama unfold. NBC, which televises the
TPC, stations ten cameras around the hole, including one on a platform in the middle of the lake. It's great theater, though Steve Lowery
undoubtedly had another, choicer, word for it in 1998 when a seagull
plucked his ball off the green and dropped it in the lake.

★ ★

If the pros have this much trouble with the 17th, you can imagine how your average hacker fares. Each year, 150,000 balls find their way into the water around the green. Since about 45,000 rounds are played each year, that averages out to slightly more than three rinsed balls per player.

The cute little 17th may look like a pussycat, but it definitely plays like a lion. For more information about the Tournament Players Club at Sawgrass go to www.tpc.com/sawgrass/ or call (904) 273-3235.

The Nazi Invasion of Florida
Ponte Vedra Beach

After the infamous September 11, 2001, attack on the United States, President George W. Bush authorized the use of military tribunals to try accused members of the al-Qaida network of terrorists. This legal tactic was controversial, but the Bush administration argued there was a direct precedent: when Nazi saboteurs landed in Florida during World War II.

Most present-day Floridians greeted this news with the same reaction: Say what?

Yet it was true, in a little-remembered incident of the great conflict. During June 1942, just six months after the surprise attack on Pearl Harbor brought the United States into the war, eight German spies slipped into the country. Nazi submarines dropped four of them off on Long Island, New York, and another four on Ponte Vedra Beach south of Jacksonville. The Germans in Florida landed in naval uniforms, then changed into civilian clothes, burying their uniforms and sabotage equipment in the sand.

(In case you ever have to play a particularly brutal level of Trivial Pursuit, Florida Edition, those Germans were Edward John Kerling, 33; Werner Thiel, 35; Herman Otto Neubauer, 32; and Herbert Hans Haupt, 22.)

The Nazi spies, who had all lived in the United States, took a bus to Jacksonville and then went by train to Cincinnati. One pair went to Chicago; the others continued to New York City. They carried more than $170,000 in cash, along with lists of contacts and targets that included department stores. The spies were betrayed by George Johann Dasch, one of those who landed on Long Island, and soon all eight were captured. Six were executed.

Michael Gannon, a history professor at the University of Florida, told the Associated Press that the saboteurs were not important. "They accomplished nothing. They were captured right away," he said. "These people truly were inconsequential, but they have piqued the American imagination."

That assessment might be a bit of a stretch. There's no historical marker commemorating the event, and locals and visitors don't think much of Nazi saboteurs, military tribunals, or the summer of '42.

Footnotes of history apparently last no longer than footprints in the sand.

Romeo, Romeo! Wherefore Art Thou, Romeo?
Romeo

Finding Romeo is easy. Take State Road 40 west from Ocala, through Martel, then bear right onto County Road 328, go about 10 miles, and you're there.

Trouble is, there's not much "there" to Romeo. Just a couple of signs on U.S. Highway 41 telling you you're entering and leaving the place. It would be just another farming community were it not for its moniker. Founded in 1850, Romeo got its name because it was just 10 miles north of Juliette. What do you think they were going to call the place? Iago?

Just like her star-crossed Shakespearean character, Juliette is no longer around. What was once Juliette is now Rainbow Springs State Park. Her name, however, lives on at Rainbow Springs Country Club, which named its restaurant after Romeo's lover.

We hear the Capulet burgers are to die for.

Photo on next page.

★ ★

Hey, many of Shakespeare's plays had sad endings, too.

In the Days before Botox
St. Augustine

Today, people turn the clock back with the help of Viagra and cosmetic surgery. But in Ponce de León's day, a simple fountain of flowing water was all that was needed to forestall the ravages of time.

★ ★

Unfortunately, the secret of eternal youthfulness was as ephemeral then as it is now.

Ancient Indian legend put the Fountain of Youth in a place called Bimini, a place north of Puerto Rico in (possibly) today's Bahama Islands. Immersing oneself in the river, spring, fountain, or whatever it was, was supposed to make the old young and the young, well . . . damp.

Juan Ponce de León (1460–1521), who had accompanied Columbus on his second voyage in 1493, is supposed to have heard of the legend from the Indians. Whether he believed it or not is another matter. (Some cynics say that Ponce de León's quest was more about gold than transmutative waters; after all, the man was only fifty-three, barely old enough for his first weave.)

In any event, Ponce de León commissioned three ships at his own expense and set out to find the Fountain of Gold . . . er, Youth. Unfortunately for him, the only thing he discovered was Florida. On March 27, 1513, Ponce de León sighted the American mainland, which, in keeping with the general perspicuity of the time, he immediately identified as an island.

Ponce de León may not have found the Fountain of Youth, but he did inspire a tourist attraction, which is almost as good. The Fountain of Youth is located in St. Augustine and is supposed to be located at the "exact spot" where the Spanish explorer staggered to shore on April 2, 1513, claiming the "New World" in the name of the king. There's lots of history to be learned at the place, and visitors can even sip from the fountain's supposedly restorative waters.

Personally, we think a healthy diet and exercise are probably better bets.

The Fountain of Youth attraction is located at 11 Magnolia Avenue in St. Augustine. Phone (904) 829-3168 or (800) 356-8222. The attraction is open from 9:00 a.m. to 5:00 p.m. Admission is $9 for adults and $5 for kids.

Excuse Me, Sir, I Mistook You for a Ghost
St. Augustine

Homeowners in St. Augustine don't brag about their new kitchens, fancy wallpaper, or high-tech TVs. They know the only sure way to impress their friends and neighbors is to boast that your home has a ghost.

To hear people talk, there are almost as many unliving walking around here as there are living. That could stem from the fact that St. Augustine, founded in 1565, is the oldest continuously occupied city in America. Over the years, the French, the Spanish, and the English have laid claim to St. Augustine, leaving behind a rich loam of international intrigue from which ghosts love to spring.

We bought a copy of *A Ghostly Experience: Tales of Saint Augustine Florida* at the bookstore next to the Oldest House, and the cashier immediately asked if we had had any personal experiences with the undead. (We haven't.) Then he went off on a long and rather predictable story about the strange noises that came from the unoccupied apartment above him, and how they only happened at night, and how he never identified their source, etc., etc. Pretty soon another cashier is chiming in about her supernatural encounter and we're still waiting for our change and it's getting late and we still haven't had any lunch.

The point of all this being that it is not hard to get the residents of St. Augustine to talk about ghosts.

But the most efficient way to learn about the city's things that go bump in the night is to take the Ghostly Experience Walking Tour. The tour begins at 8:00 p.m. nightly next to the Oldest Wooden Schoolhouse (everything in St. Augustine is the oldest something-or-other) and lasts an hour and a half. During that time, a guide dressed in a monk's robe or some other "period" outfit leads a group of fifteen or so down some of the city's dark, narrow streets, past cemeteries and old houses that no self-respecting haunt could pass up.

Our guide, Michael, halted us beside the St. Francis Inn at 279 St. George Street. (St. George Street, by the way, is like an interstate highway for ghosts. It looks like something straight out of a Harry Potter book.) Then he told us the story of the nephew of a military officer who fell in love with one of the house servants in the middle part of the nineteenth century. The couple would sneak up into the attic (now room 3-A) to, as Michael says with a wink, "hold hands." The uncle discovered them and furiously sent the servant away, instructing his nephew that he was never to see her again.

Broken-hearted, the nephew hanged himself in the attic.

Today, it is believed that the ghost of the young servant, named Lily, has taken up residence in room 3-A. While cleaning the room, a housekeeper turned on the TV to keep her company. She went out to the hallway to get some bed linens and when she returned, the TV was switched off.

The housekeeper's line, allegedly, was that "Lily doesn't like MTV."

If you think tourists would go out of their way to avoid staying in room 3-A, you don't understand the "spirit" of St. Augustine. Reservations are booked a year in advance, and some tourists refuse to leave until they see an apparition or a piece of furniture moving by itself.

They not only ain't afraid of no ghosts in St. Augustine, most places are accepting applications.

The seventy-five-minute Ghostly Experience Walking Tour meets next to the City Gates at 8:00 p.m. A second tour begins at 9:30 p.m. on Friday and Saturday nights. Phone (888) 461-1009 for more details, including ticket prices.

She Loves Me, She Loves Me Knot
St. Augustine

On Orange Street, near the intersection of Cordova Street, is a strange thing of the botanical kind.

In the front yard of a private residence, a palm tree is growing out of the trunk of an oak tree. Both trees are full-grown and appear quite healthy, or at least as healthy as something can appear that has another thing growing out of its body.

The legend of St. Augustine's Love Tree
is more romantic than the reality.

★ ★

Perhaps because they are intertwined so inextricably, the duo is called the Love Tree. Legend has it that if a guy and a gal kiss in the shadow of the Love Tree, they will be frozen in a tomb of wood forever with birds pooping on their heads and termites gnawing on their hindquarters.

Wait. That's a different legend. Ah, yes. This legend says that the kissing couple will remain in love to their dying day.

Or until someone cuts the Love Tree down to make room for a condo. Whichever comes first.

This Really Old House
St. Augustine

There are only two things wrong with the Gonzalez-Alvarez House's claim to be the Oldest House:

No one knows exactly how old it is.
It's not the Oldest House.

What the building at 14 St. Francis Street is, is (probably) the oldest continuously occupied house in the oldest continuously occupied city in America. Our tour guide pointed out that some houses in New England are older, as is an adobe hut in New Mexico.

But these are nothing more than annoying quibbles in a town that boasts of not only having the Oldest House, but also the Oldest Wooden Schoolhouse and the Oldest Drug Store. (We stayed in a motel that quite possibly had the Oldest Plumbing, but that claim has not yet been authenticated.)

Still, there is no doubt that the Oldest House is very, very old. Archaeologists claim that some sort of building has been continuously occupied on the Oldest House site since the early 1600s. The building that tourists visit today is the same, more or less, as the building that was rebuilt after British troops burned St. Augustine to the ground for the second time in 1702.

A modern real estate agent would probably describe the Oldest

★ ★

This is believed to be the oldest house in the United States by everyone except those who say it isn't.

House as a "fixer-upper." The original bottom floor consisted of two rooms in which eight people lived. There was no glass in the windows (too expensive), and a brazier in the middle of the floor of the main room was kept continuously stoked—in the winter to provide heat and in the summer to smoke away mosquitoes. Bedding consisted of a thin straw mat unfurled over a floor of tabby, a concretelike mixture of lime, shell, and sand.

Our guide said that the house was typical of how the "upper middle class" lived in St. Augustine in the early 1700s. Those less well-off presumably stayed in our motel.

One of the earliest known occupants of the Oldest House was Tomas Gonzalez y Hernandez, an artilleryman at the nearby fort.

✮ ✮

When Spain ceded Florida to England in 1763, the town's 3,000 Spanish residents, including Gonzalez and his family, had to leave.

The house changed hands several times and was eventually bought at auction in 1790 by Geronimo Alvarez. He and his descendants lived in the house for more than one hundred years, adding a second story and furnishings that look positively modern compared to what's going on on the floor below.

The Oldest House, like just about every other building in St. Augustine built before 1980, is said to be haunted by ghosts. We didn't meet any, but we didn't volunteer to spend the night either.

The Oldest House is located at 271 Charlotte Street. Next to it is the Tovar House, another extremely old house, and a military museum that displays weapons dating back hundreds of years. For more information call (904) 824-2872 or visit the website at www.staugustine historicalsociety.org.

Land of 1,000 Gators

St. Augustine

There are no roller coasters at St. Augustine Alligator Farm Zoological Park, nor any plummeting elevators or things that spin you around until you lose your lunch.

The place is basically about alligators. Lots of alligators. More than 1,000 of them and their crocodile cousins. The biggest is Baby Huey, a 13-foot gator that weighs more than 900 pounds. Baby Huey doesn't put on much of a show. In fact, he mostly just lies there, soaking up the sun and looking dead. You, as a tourist, are supposed to look at Baby Huey and say, "Whoa! That is one big gator! Do you think it's alive?"

That was about all the entertainment value visitors used to need or expect from Florida tourist attractions before the D-word arrived in Orlando and changed everything. The Alligator Farm, one of Florida's oldest tourist attractions, has been in operation since the early 1890s. The fact that it's still around testifies to the fact that some people still

★ ★

prefer a real, if somnambulant, gator to a hyperactive animatronic mouse.

The pens and ponds in which the gators live give off a swampy smell, another clue that you are not in the land of the plastic rodent. This is not to say that the Alligator Farm does not have a sense of whimsy. On an island on which numerous 10-foot alligators roam is a sign that reads NO TRESPASSING!

Understandably, the attraction doesn't find it necessary to post guards to keep people from jumping the fence.

There are other interesting critters at the park besides alligators and crocodiles. We particularly enjoyed the Galapagos tortoises,

This No Trespassing sign seems unnecessary.

which can live to be 200 years old and weigh more than 600 pounds. Looking like reptilian Volkswagens, the tortoises lumber along, munching grass and lettuce given to them by their keepers. Compared to the gators and crocs, these guys seem like roadrunners.

The best time to visit the Alligator Farm is in the late afternoon when flocks of blue herons, white egrets, ibis, and wood storks return from a day of feeding to the rookery at the attraction. When we visited, in March, the egrets were decked out in their mating plumage, lacy white tail feathers that hunters used to collect for women's hats, bringing the species to the verge of extinction.

Also, don't miss the show at the Reptile Theater, where handler Shannon Chapman will let you pet her friend, Chip the alligator.

No need to be afraid. Chip's mouth is taped shut.

With Scotch tape.

The Alligator Farm Zoological Park is located on State Road A1A just across the Bridge of Lions from St. Augustine. The park is open daily from 9:00 a.m. to 5:00 p.m. Phone (904) 824-3337 for more information. Admission is charged.

Damn Yankees

Yankeetown

Not many Florida towns like to admit to ties with the accursed "Nawth," but Yankeetown is an exception. A tiny Gulf Coast hamlet of about 640 souls in Levy County, Yankeetown was founded in the early 1920s by A. F. Knotts, a Gary, Indiana, lawyer who loved hunting and fishing. Knotts bought 2,000 acres along the Withlachoochee River and built the Izaak Walton Lodge, named after the famous seventeenth-century author and outdoorsman. Knotts' northern friends flocked to the place (the original snowbirds, perhaps?) to the point that the locals began referring to the camp as "the place where all the Yankees go."

The town, such as it is, was incorporated in 1924 and the name stuck. The fishing, by the way, remains excellent.

Gomek the Magnificent

Once upon a time, a long time ago, there was born in New Guinea a little crocodile by the name of . . .

Actually, the little crocodile didn't have a name because it was . . . well, little. But the little crocodile grew and grew and grew until it was very big and it started eating natives the way you or I might eat popcorn shrimp at Red Lobster. Local villagers gave the big croc a name. They called it "Crocodile You Don't Want to Let in Your Restaurant on All-You-Can-Eat-Natives Fridays." No, we're making that up. They called the critter Louma, "crocodile inhabited by evil spirits."

In 1968 a trapper by the name of George Craig captured Louma. At 17½ feet and 2,000 pounds, he was proclaimed the largest crocodile in captivity. Louma, for reasons that are not entirely clear, was renamed Gomek, after an Australian comic book character. Presumably the name "Charlie Brown" was already taken.

Anyway, Gomek spent some time wowing crowds in Australia and Indonesia before winding up at the St. Augustine Alligator Farm in 1989. It didn't take long for Gomek to become the attraction's Celebrity Croc. Gomek had his own (large) pool at the Alligator Farm and chose from a daily menu that included mullet, chicken, and smaller crocs too slow or too stupid to stay out of his way. Despite his ferocious reputation, Gomek's handlers described the huge Indopacific crocodile as docile and a good husband, in the sense that in the eight years he was at the Alligator Farm, he never once devoured his crocodile mate, Anna Bell.

Alas, the soft life proved Gomek's undoing; he died in 1997 of a heart attack, presumably from failing to remove the skin from his chicken.

But Gomek lives on, at least in taxidermy heaven. His enormous stuffed carcass is ensconced in its own shrinelike house on the grounds of the Alligator Farm. Believed to have been between sixty and eighty years old at the time of his death, Gomek is posed in a decidedly undocile stance, with his huge mouth agape and his feet ready to run down the most uncooperative chicken and/or villager.

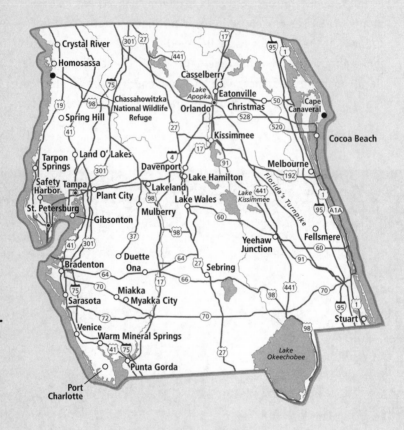

Crystal River
301 27
Homosassa
17
441 95 1
Casselberry
75 Lake Eatonville
Chassahowitzka Apopka Cape
National Wildlife Orlando Christmas 50 Canaveral
Refuge 528
19 98 520
Spring Hill 27 Cocoa Beach
41 Kissimmee
Land O' Lakes Davenport 17 91 Melbourne
Tarpon 4 192
Springs 301 Lake Hamilton Florida's Turnpike
Safety Lakeland 1
Harbor Tampa Plant City Lake Kissimmee 95 A1A
98 Lake Wales
St. Petersburg 60
Gibsonton Mulberry 98
41 301 37 98 Fellsmere
Duette 64 Yeehaw 60
Bradenton Ona Junction 91
64 27
70 Sebring 441 70
Sarasota Miakka 17 66 98 95 1
72 Myakka City 70 Stuart
Venice 70
Warm Mineral Springs 98
41 75 27 Lake
Punta Gorda Okeechobee
Port
Charlotte

Central Florida

Central Florida

Central Florida is *the unquestioned domain of Mickey Mouse, Shamu and their kin at the area's mega-theme parks. If you're looking for front-porch swings and solitude, you've definitely come too far south.*

Greater Orlando—the home of Disney World, SeaWorld Orlando and Universal Studios Florida—is a major tourism hub. More than forty-eight million people visited the area in 2008 (exact figures are a closely guarded secret), which means that people, even in these dire economic times, can still scrape together enough cash to visit the Magic Kingdom, www.disneyworld.disney.go.com. (They can also scrape together enough cash to visit the Hard Rock Hotel and Casino in Tampa, www .seminolehardrocktampa.com, but that is another story.)

Don't visit Orlando if you like to tool around in your car. The area is known locally as The Land of Everlasting Road Construction, much of it taking place on perhaps the most evil highway in Florida, Interstate 4. Wherever you are going in Central Florida, try to get there without taking this road. Use a map, a GPS, a Seminole Indian guide . . . whatever it takes to avoid this traffic nightmare. (There are many alternate routes to Disney World. Use them.)

If you can tear yourself away from the theme parks, Central Florida has a lot to offer. Northwest of Orlando is Crystal River (www.crystal riverflorida.com), where you can swim with manatees (as of this writing) or at least view them close-up from slow-moving boats. (Boat propellers are the scourge of Florida's manatee population.) If that sounds too adventurous, you can travel south to Bradenton and say hi to Snooty (www.southfloridamuseum.org), the world's oldest captive-born manatee, located in, appropriately enough, Manatee County.

If you want a taste of what Florida attractions used to be pre-Disney, visit Sarasota Jungle Gardens (www.sarasotajunglegardens.com). Take in the parrot show and then enjoy a leisurely stroll beneath the cool, green canopy of the "jungle," which leads to Flamingo Lake, a photo opportunity if there ever was one. (Don't pass up the gift shop, a wonderfully tacky reminder of Old Florida.)

Then travel east into the interior of Central Florida, which has a lot more to do with strawberry fields, tomato fields and phosphate mines than it does with scary water rides. To learn more about Florida's giant (and controversial) phosphate industry, visit the Phosphate Museum in Mulberry (www.mulberrychamber.org). The narrative is all from the phosphate industry's point of view (hey, somebody's got to pay for the exhibits), but you'll get a better understanding of what role fertilizer plays in our daily lives (toothpaste, for instance).

Mickey may be the 800-pound rodent in Central Florida, but there's a lot more to the region than mice.

The Best Argument against Vegetarianism Yet
Bradenton

What's old and gray and likes to float nude on his back in his swimming pool while women rub his belly and feed him bite-size chunks of fruit?

No, not Hugh Hefner (but that's a good guess). It's Snooty the manatee, the official mascot and namesake of Manatee County. At sixty-one, Snooty is the oldest living manatee born in captivity. A lifelong bachelor, Snooty cruises (cavorts would be too strong a word at his age) around the 60,000-gallon Parker Manatee Aquarium in the South Florida Museum in downtown Bradenton.

Snooty maintains his svelte 1,000-pound figure by adhering to a strict vegetarian diet. Lettuce, carrots, and apples disappear into his whiskered snout at the rate of eighty pounds a day. He is also partial to sweet potatoes, broccoli, strawberries, and monkey chow. (No word on whether monkeys enjoy a snack of manatee chow.)

Snooty's handlers cater to Snooty's every need, including the aforementioned belly rubs and back scrubs. Thousands of schoolchildren troop through the aquarium every year for Snooty's birthday party and to learn more about this endangered species.

Wildlife experts estimate there are only about 2,500 manatees in Florida waters, and more than 200 die every year, chiefly from injuries suffered from boat propellers.

Although Snooty is definitely a tourist attraction who loves playing to the crowds, he also serves a valuable educational purpose. The children who fall in love with the docile mammal are the same children who will tell their parents to slow down their boats in waters known to contain manatees.

(Snooty's public relations value skyrocketed when someone had the good sense to change his original name, which was Stinky, and to trademark his new name.)

If you visit Snooty, don't be surprised if he has a pool mate. Injured or orphaned manatees sometimes spend a few months at the Parker

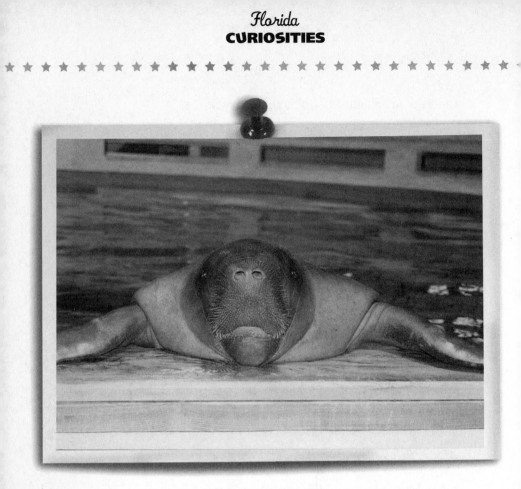

With a face only a mother manatee could love, Snooty, at sixty-one, is the oldest living captive manatee.

Manatee Aquarium before being reintroduced to the wild. Snooty, however, isn't going anywhere. After all, monkey chow doesn't grow on trees.

The Parker Manatee Aquarium is located at 201 Tenth Street, Bradenton. The phone number is (941) 746-4131; you can also visit online at www.southfloridamuseum.org. Admission is charged. Aquarium hours are 8:00 a.m. to 5:00 p.m. Monday through Saturday and 10:00 a.m. to 5:00 p.m. on Sunday.

The Spirit of Christmas
Brooksville

Perhaps the sensory overload of rooms full of decorated trees, ornaments and other Christmas-related doodads caused some people's imaginations to run wild.

But lately the iconic Rogers' Christmas House & Village in Brooksville is almost as well-known for its hauntings as it is for its impressive inventory of holiday decorations.

The Village consists of five small cottages dating back to 1887. Experts in this sort of thing say that the age of a building is very important to ghosts. Perhaps it's union rules or simply architectural snobbishness; we can't really say. In any event, things that go bump in the night clearly feel right at home in this place. There have been reports of mysterious toilet flushings, specters peering out of windows and, our personal favorite, a translucent man who sits on a bench outside one of the cottages playing a clarinet.

We didn't see any ghosts when we visited, nor did we see many customers, which is probably more alarming to management than the haunts. In the 1970s and 1980s the Christmas House, which is open every day except Christmas, was a bustling place. Nearly half a million people visited each year, coming from such faraway places as Mogadishu, Morocco and Berlin. Sadly, the Christmas House fell upon hard times, the nadir being a 2008 bankruptcy involving then-owner Donna Jones. Business dried up as many people assumed the Christmas House had closed for good.

Hoping to revitalize the place are Matt Senge and Karen Hyde, who recently moved to Brooksville from Alexandria, Virginia. Collectors of unique Christmas ornaments, the couple visited the place after seeing a sign on Interstate 75. Karen fell in love with the charm and fantasy of the Christmas House and told her husband she'd like to own a place like that some day.

Matt Senge has ambitious plans for the place, including a deli, a tearoom and eventually a fine dining restaurant behind the main

Rogers' Christmas House and Village
celebrates the holiday year-round.

building. The vast array of Christmas stuff will be squeezed into two or three cottages, making way for the renovations.

The couple have many obstacles to overcome, not the least of which is the lousy Florida economy. They also have to worry about the guy on the bench playing a clarinet. Ghosts, as a rule, don't cotton to change.

Rogers' Christmas House & Village is located at 103 South Saxon Avenue in Brooksville. It is open every day except Christmas from 9:30 a.m. to 5 p.m. The toll-free phone number is (877) 312-5046, or visit www.rogerschristmashouse.com.

The Space Shuttle Shuffles into History
Cape Canaveral

By the end of 2010, the Kennedy Space Center and surrounding Cape Canaveral will be a sadder and decidedly less prosperous place.

The last of 134 Space Shuttle missions is scheduled to lift off in November, bringing to a close forty-nine years of manned U.S. space flight. Future astronauts who make the trip to the International Space Station will do so atop a Russian-built Soyuz rocket (or perhaps a launch vehicle made in China or a privately owned spacecraft). They will be paying passengers and the fare is expected to be in the neighborhood of $50 million per seat. (One hopes, at a minimum, that they get free peanuts and a pillow.)

Those of us of a certain age can be forgiven if we wax nostalgic about that spring day in 1961 when we huddled around our elementary school teacher's black-and-white TV to watch, in awe and terror, as Alan Shepard's Freedom 7 rocket ship rose slowly—so slowly!—from its launch pad, white smoke and hellish flames billowing outward, the thin, metal tube's upward rise as unstoppable and unpredictable as a bullet leaving the barrel of a gun. Walter Cronkite was there, of course, and he reassured us, of course, even though he had no more idea than we did as to how it would all turn out and if the brave, if somewhat cocky, man sitting atop the giant candle would live to be a hero or simply go "poof" in front of millions of Americans, including schoolchildren who had yet to grasp long division.

A lot of things happened after that, some good, some bad. But space flight always seemed to be something that drew us together as a people. After all, if you can't get excited about one of your country-men walking on the moon, you really ought to check and see if you have a pulse.

But after the moon landing in 1969, NASA's mission grew fuzzier, at least in the minds of the American people. The space program was expensive. Couldn't the money be better spent here on Earth? And what was the purpose of the International Space Station, other than to provide a destination for our Space Shuttles?

The technology grew more sophisticated but the danger remained. Fourteen astronauts lost their lives on Space Shuttle missions, seven on the Challenger on January 28, 1986, and seven on the Colum-bia on February 1, 2003. America's space program was reeling even before the recession sent it to the mat.

The Space Shuttle Endeavour, predicted to touch ground in November 2010, will not only bring to a close an important chapter in American history; at least 7,000 jobs will be lost at Kennedy Space Center alone.

So much for happy endings.

Where It's Christmas All the Time

Christmas

Florida might not be the first state that comes to mind when you think of Christmas. (The palm trees, warm weather, and decided lack of snow might have something to do with this.) But that doesn't mean the Sunshine State lacks the Christmas spirit.

There is a small town in Orange County that is actually called Christmas. In the 1930s, the post office near Fort Christmas began adding Christmas tree postmarks to letters. Today, during the holiday season, about 250,000 pieces of mail are sent through the post office from people desiring that postmark.

Since the 1970s, the Kennedy Space Center has made a shuttle landing strip available on Christmas Eve for Santa Claus "in the event of a reindeer problem or mechanical difficulty." (So far, Santa has completed his rounds without having to make an emergency landing.)

Florida also is a player in the Christmas-tree business. More than 120,000 trees are shipped from the state each year.

And did you know that the first Christmas mass in America was celebrated in 1539 near what is now Tallahassee by Spanish conquistador Hernando de Soto?

Just because snow doesn't often fall from the sky in Florida doesn't mean we can't make some. The city of Kissimmee holds an annual Holiday Extravaganza on its lakefront that features rides, games, a lighted parade, and, yes, twenty tons of honest-to-goodness snow.

Or at least its manufactured equivalent.

For more information on the Holiday Extravaganza, call (407) 933-8368.

Florida's 24-Hour Surf Shop
Cocoa Beach

The Ron Jon Surf Shop, a Cocoa Beach institution for nearly fifty years, has stores throughout the state and across the country, with plans to expand into Canada and Central America. It's one of the best-recognized brands on the beach. The flagship store is open twenty-four hours a day.

If you want to buy a surfboard at midnight, or replace your wet suit at 3:00 a.m., this is the place.

Ron Jon has hundreds of surfboards on display, but the 50,000-square-foot store sells more clothing than anything else. A great majority of customers are tourists, not surfers, and a great number of their purchases are Ron Jon souvenirs. The shop offers an astonishing array of stuff. Ron Jon shorts, T-shirts, and jackets. Ron

★ ★

Jon caps, hats, and visors. Ron Jon ashtrays, shot glasses, and insulated cups. Ron Jon backpacks, tote bags, and beach towels. Ron Jon postcards, key chains, and refrigerator magnets. Even Ron Jon gift cards and mouse pads.

You get the idea.

Ron Jon billboards throughout the state offer the mileage to the Cocoa Beach shop. For years local residents used the signs to estimate how long it would take them to drive home. Even on the Gulf Coast, Floridians know the name. "The Ron Jon Story," printed in store brochures, tells how young Ron DiMenna, a New Jersey surfer, wanted to order a custom board from California. His dad told him to order three and sell two, getting his own board for free. After opening the original Ron Jon Surf Shop on the Jersey shore, DiMenna expanded to Cocoa Beach in 1963.

Since then the Florida business has grown in size, sales, and stature. The sign out front says One of a Kind. Besides selling beach clothes and equipment, Ron Jon rents out surfboards and kayaks. There's a surf school at a nearby beach. Now there's even a Ron Jon Resort in Cape Canaveral.

In 2006, though, the Brevard County store got something new—local competition in excess. The Cocoa Beach Surf Company moved next door on Atlantic Avenue, determined to outdo the original in every way. It's billed as "The World's Largest Surf Complex," with three floors of merchandise, an escalator, and a 60-foot-tall atrium. It's connected to a Sheraton hotel. There's a saltwater aquarium and a Starbucks, too.

The Surf Company is only open from 8:00 a.m. to 11:00 p.m., though, so Ron Jon remains the only twenty-four-hour surf shop in town.

The Ron Jon Surf Shop is at 4151 N. Atlantic Avenue in Cocoa Beach. Visit www.ronjonsurfshop.com or call (321) 799-8888.

✳ ✳

The Ron Jon Surf Shop in Cocoa Beach is famous throughout Florida. The 50,000-square-foot store is open twenty-four hours a day.

Weddings on the Water

Cortez

The Floating Chapel on the Bay is such a good idea that you just want to kick yourself for not having thought of it first.

Advertised as America's only self-propelled floating chapel, the spiffy blue-and-white church sits atop twin pontoons and motors (very slowly) around Sarasota Bay and Anna Maria Sound thanks to a pair of 125-horsepower engines.

The inside of the 100-seat chapel looks a lot like a land-locked church except for the life preservers stowed under the pews. The stained-glass windows, the plum carpeting and the vaulted ceiling suggest a grandeur that belies the boat's relatively small size (60 feet by 30 feet).

According to event coordinator Jill Chandler-Fisher, weddings account for most of the chapel's business, but the boat can be booked for a variety of functions including wedding anniversaries, vow renewals, and commitment ceremonies.

People who elect to get married in a floating chapel tend to be whimsical by nature, Chandler-Fisher said. One couple dressed up their pet boxer and shih tzu in tuxedos and included them in the ceremony. (We don't know which one got to kiss the bride first.)

Wedding cruises take about two hours and cost anywhere from $1,000 to $3,000 depending on the size of the group and the distance traveled. Couples are invited to bring their own champagne for toasting purposes, but don't plan on releasing any balloons or butterflies. Chandler-Fisher, a self-described environmentalist, doesn't want to run the risk of any animals getting hurt.

Chandler-Fisher's husband, Capt. Orca Fisher (no, we're not making this name up) conducts many of the wedding ceremonies, but couples can make their own arrangements if they wish.

As you might imagine, the sight of a steepled church motoring down the Intercoastal Waterway can be a bit of a traffic stopper. Motorists invariably toot their horns when the boat passes beneath the Cortez Road drawbridge and fishermen interrupt their pursuit of snook and redfish to hoot and holler.

It all makes for a memorable and delightful wedding day, assuming no one gets seasick.

For more information on the Floating Chapel on the Bay, phone (941) 379-7327 or visit www.weddingsonwater.com.

✭ ✭

Lightning Striking Again
Crystal Beach

Don Naumann is no different from any other person who keeps a lightning detector next to his bed.

Naumann has been photographing lightning since 1991. He only shoots at night, which is why the lightning detector comes in handy.

"It seems like all the best storms happen around 3 a.m.," he said shaking his head.

Naumann scouts out promising locations by pedaling around the shoreline on his bicycle. He is often accompanied by his five-year-old black Labrador retriever, Marlee. Marlee doesn't have much interest in lightning but she loves swimming in the bay, even in the winter when the water temperature drops into the 40s.

"She's nuts," Naumann said. (Marlee wouldn't say whether she shared the same opinion as her owner.)

A professional photographer whose work has appeared in art galleries around the country, Naumann decided to shoot lightning bolts because he was bored with more conventional subject matter.

"When I started, I didn't realize how dangerous lightning can be. I learned real quick," he said.

His moment of illumination, so to speak, came when he was watching an approaching thunderstorm from what he thought was the safety of a friend's front porch.

"The bolt hit a tree about 100 feet from me, but the force knocked me backward through a screen door. I was scared to death."

Naumann learned to take his lightning detector with him on shoots. When the alarm goes off, he knows the storm is within a couple of miles and that it's time to pack up his camera and tripod and run to the car.

It takes patience to be a good lightning photographer. His most popular photo, called "The Wreck," took two years and fifty trips to make.

"A lot of it is luck," he admitted. "Sometimes I don't realize I've got a good shot until I get the photos back from the processor."

Don Naumann's lightning photos sometimes are two years in the making.
COURTESY OF DON NAUMANN

Naumann captures his images on film, using timed exposures of anywhere from ten seconds to ten minutes. The camera he uses is a 1959 Hasselblad with a 50-millimeter lens. The 2¼ inch by 2¼ inch format allows him to enlarge the images with minimal loss of clarity. Prints of his work can be purchased over the Internet and cost anywhere from $20 to $550.

Naumann, 61, has been slowed a little lately by hip replacement surgery but he still keeps an eye out for good shooting locations. He says he'd like to travel around the country shooting lightning, but for the time being he's content with the awesome shows that occur, literally, in his own backyard.

"Nothing beats the west coast of Florida," he said. "It's not called the lightning capital of the world for nothing."

Don Naumann can be reached by phone at (727) 518-4492. His website is www.dnlightning.com.

Whoop! There It Is!
Crystal River

If you looked up at the sky above Chassahowitzka National Wildlife Refuge last fall, you might have thought to yourself: Wow! That's one hard-to-pronounce national wildlife refuge!

But that would have been stupid. What you should have thought was that you were witnessing a scene out of the movie *Fly Away Home.*

A flock of large birds, flying in formation, was gamely following an ultralight airplane piloted by a guy in a white suit. The birds were whooping cranes, and they were on the last leg of a 1,300-mile journey that began at Necedah National Wildlife Refuge in Wisconsin.

The odd procession was the first step in building what will hopefully be the first self-sustaining colony of whoopers in Florida and the second in the nation. In the 1940s, due to overhunting and loss of habitat, only fifteen birds remained. Life got better for North

★ ★

America's largest bird when then-President Franklin D. Roosevelt created the Aransas National Wildlife Refuge out of 47,000 acres of marsh and forest in Texas. That colony now consists of more than 150 whoopers. (Can you tell we love using the word *whoopers*?)

Scientists discovered that whooping cranes lay two eggs each year, but only one survives. That allowed them to take one egg from each nest and artificially hatch it. The only problem was that there were no adult whoopers around to lead the young birds south for the winter.

That's when the idea of the ultralight airplane was born. The chicks' keepers, wearing white jumpsuits so as to resemble (sort of) momma, played recordings of the airplane's propeller noise to the babies before they hatched. When born, the chicks were not afraid of the airplanes and were willing to follow them into the air.

Why ultralights? They're the only aircraft that can fly slow enough—about 35 miles per hour—for the cranes to keep up.

Even so, the flight south was no day in the swamp. The birds and their gas-powered mother averaged only 30 miles a day, and storms were frequent.

The birds, only seven months old when they arrived at the 30,000-acre Chassahowitzka Refuge, are free to come and go as they please, leaving open the possibility of more losses. They seem to be comfortable in their new surroundings though, according to Chuck Underwood of the U.S. Fish and Wildlife Service, and they spend their days feasting on blue crabs, snails, and small fish.

Come spring, the whoopers will (hopefully) be able to find their way back to Wisconsin on their own, without an ultralight escort. A fresh batch of birds will be chaperoned down south every fall for the next few years until a self-sustaining breeding colony of the 5-foot-tall cranes is established.

Until then, if you look skyward at the right time of year, you might be treated to the rare sight of a flock of whooping cranes and their sputtering momma heading south for the winter.

(Whoopers, whoopers, whoopers.)

★ ★

At present, the public is not allowed to get up close and personal with the whooping cranes, but that policy is expected to relax once the colony establishes itself. For more information, call the park at (352) 563-2088. The refuge's headquarters are located at 1520 S.E. Kings Bay Drive, Crystal River, and online at www.fws.gov/chassahowitzka.

Hang Gliders Soar over Wallaby Ranch
Davenport

There are no wallabies at Wallaby Ranch. No kangaroos or koalas either, mate. There is hang gliding, though, lots of hang gliding. The sport was invented in Australia, which means it all makes sense in a soaring sort of way west of Orlando.

On a clear day, pilots can see all the way to Walt Disney World.

Wallaby Ranch is billed as the world's largest full-time hang-gliding club, but it might also be the best-kept secret in central Florida. Directions to the place lead to a mailbox—yes, a mailbox—along lonely State Road 54 near Clermont. There you'll find a tiny sign, along with a bumper sticker that reads HANG-GLIDER PILOT: I BRAKE FOR BIRDS. For owner Malcolm Jones, Wallaby Ranch is his Shangri-La, and business is just about right.

"It's mostly word of mouth," he says. "You don't see blinking lights out there. We're not trying to be Gatorland. It's sort of a commune we have here. We live here; this is our home.

"It's like our little oasis of hang-gliding hippiedom," Jones explains. "It actually isn't as hippie as it used to be, when everything was cheaper, but the camaraderie's quick and strong."

Hang gliding is usually associated with mountains, where pilots can launch off cliffs, but Wallaby Ranch was one of the pioneers in aero-towing, using ultralight airplanes to tow gliders into the sky. The wry "Fine Print" section of the Wallaby Ranch brochure includes a cross section of slogans, advice, and philosophies of life for visiting pilots:

"Have fun, relax. Be cool, get a T-shirt. Stay upwind. Don't land in the orange grove next door. No whiners! Try to remember to

★ ★

pay—sometimes we forget to ask. Remember that we are a club, not an industry. Share in the positive energy of the Ranch lifestyle. Peace."

After a visit to Australia, Jones decided to name his Florida camp for the cuddly Australian animal. It was more of a personal than a business decision.

"I didn't want to call it the ABC Flight Center, you know?" he says. "Originally, I wanted to have wallabies out here."

That plan ended when it turned out that the animals are scared to death—literally—of dogs. They would have had to be kept in a walled cage that kind of defeated the purpose of the whole idea.

There is hang gliding at Wallaby Ranch, though, lots of hang gliding.

Wallaby Ranch is at 1805 Dean Still Road, Davenport. Tandem discovery flights, student certification packages, glider rentals, and flying club rates are offered. For details visit www.wallaby.com or call (863) 424-0070 or (800) WALLABY.

Airstream Art
Dover

As you're proceeding east on I-4 toward Orlando, your eye may catch sight of eight upended Airstream RVs tilting skyward in a possible homage to Cadillac Ranch in Amarillo, Texas, or, equally likely, an unsubtle advertisement for the nearby Bates RV Exchange.

The "artistic" display is the brainchild of RV Exchange owner Frank Bates, who swears he was so inspired by Cadillac Ranch that he named his 2008 composition Airstream Ranch. His argument has been somewhat sullied by the fact that the elderly, reflective Airstreams look better from the highway than they do from the windows of nearby homes. All of which has brought into question the issue of art versus kitsch, a subject the Hillsborough County judiciary has been loath to address. We do not pretend to have any insight into this matter other than to say that this is Florida and if tackiness were a crime, half the population would be in jail.

So, for now, the Airstream Ranch will remain as it is, except that Bates, who apparently does not know when to quit, plans to install floodlights and palm trees to bring more attention to his installation. Future modifications include the addition of a Muffler Man, something the builders of Stonehenge somehow overlooked.

While we appreciate the novelty of eight somewhat dilapidated Airstream trailers buried nose-first into the ground, we strongly discourage you from stopping alongside busy I-4 to photograph the sight. Better, by far, to pay a visit to Bates RV Exchange at 4656 McIntosh Road in Dover. Not only will you reduce your chances of becoming road kill, but the helpful people in the office will either direct you to a footpath or, depending on the weather, suggest you purchase one or more of the reasonably priced postcards.

And if you want to buy a new Airstream, so much the better.

The Airstream Ranch is located just to the west of exit 14 on eastbound I-4. For more information call Bates RV Exchange at (813) 659-0008. Their website is www.batesrv.com.

Don't Talk, Just Duette

Duette

One might quibble whether it's actually a one-room schoolhouse (a classroom and an adjoining auditorium/lunchroom are connected by a door), but Duette Elementary is unquestionably Florida's last one-teacher schoolhouse.

For many years, that teacher has been Donna King, or "Miss Donna" as she's lovingly known to her students, who until recently numbered about fifteen. But with Manatee County's population continually pushing eastward, the little school is now bursting with students.

Duette Elementary is an odd mixture of the old and the new. Volunteers built the building in 1930 when Albritton, Bunker Hill, and Duette schools were consolidated into one. The green chalkboards and tongue-and-groove wooden interior walls definitely belong to an earlier day. For

★ ★

many years, Duette Elementary, which once taught students through the eighth grade, was considered a "strawberry school" because there were no classes during the strawberry picking season from January to March.

Today, despite its remote location (it's 25 miles to the nearest full-size elementary school), Duette Elementary is a technological front-runner. Every student has his or her own computer, compared to the average of one computer for every three students in other Manatee County schools.

While some teachers might be daunted by the prospect of teaching grades kindergarten through five in one room at the same time, Miss Donna enjoys the challenge, as is evidenced by several Teacher of the Year nominations.

Because of its size and remoteness, it costs more to educate Duette Elementary students than it does students at bigger schools. The subject of shutting down the little school comes before the local school board every now and then, but so far local residents have managed to keep the school open, even if they've had to dig into their own pockets.

Duette Elementary School is located at the corner of State Road 62 and Keenton Road, 18 miles east of U.S. Highway 301, in rural eastern Manatee County. The phone number is (941) 721-6674. The website is www.manatee.k12.fl.us.

Florida's First Incorporated Black Town
Eatonville

Zora Neale Hurston, one of Florida's foremost authors, took pride in her home north of Orlando: "I was born in a Negro town. I do not mean by that the black back-side of an average town. Eatonville, Florida, is, and was at the time of my birth, a pure Negro town—charter, mayor, council, town marshal, and all. It was not the first Negro community in America, but it was the first to be incorporated, the first attempt at organized self-government on the part of Negroes in America."

Eatonville, founded in 1887, survives as a predominantly black community of about 2,000 people. Hurston, who was born in 1891 and died in 1960, is remembered in a namesake Museum of Fine Arts, along with an annual arts festival called Zora!

The Eatonville novelist went on to write *Jonah's Gourd Vine* and *Their Eyes Were Watching God,* along with an autobiography, *Dust Tracks on a Road.* Her books include hometown descriptions of the local general store and the "lying porch" where townspeople gathered.

Hurston's father, John, a minister and master carpenter, was an Alabama native drawn to Florida by the promise of a new settlement. The *Eatonville Speaker* newspaper offered notices such as this one on January 22, 1889: "Colored people of the United States—Solve the great race problem by securing a home in Eatonville, Florida, a Negro city governed by Negroes." Local accomplishments included the Hungerford School, modeled after the Tuskegee Institute, along with the Macedonia Missionary Baptist Church.

Both remain today, after a fashion, and both are part of a walking tour of the town sponsored by the Association to Preserve the Eatonville Community. What was the Old Apopka Road, and then Eatonville Road, is now Kennedy Boulevard. Plaques around town point out old pathways, cemeteries, and citrus groves.

For more information on Eatonville, call the town offices at (407) 623-1313. For more information on Historic Eatonville, call (407) 647-3307.

Birthplace of Equal Suffrage
Fellsmere

Fellsmere might be a forgotten town on a forlorn road between Melbourne and Fort Pierce, but it claims a proud place in Florida history. On June 19, 1915, Mrs. Zena M. Dreier voted in a city election. She was the first woman in Florida—indeed, the first woman south of the Mason-Dixon Line—to cast a municipal ballot.

A year later, the *Fellsmere Tribune* congratulated itself on having fine readers and worthy citizens: "The population of Fellsmere is of

★ ★

a high type of intelligence, with lofty ideals and wise execution. Progressive in all things, perhaps no better indication of the fact may be given than the unanimous vote of the town granting unrestricted suffrage to women."

In 1920, the Nineteenth Amendment to the Constitution gave all American women the right to vote, but this was only following the example of Fellsmere.

The perfect place to contemplate this idea might be the Marsh Landing Restaurant on Broadway Street in Fellsmere. The walls are lined with cypress panels from the 1920s. The table tops are decorated with old copies of the *Fellsmere Farmer* and *Fellsmere Tribune*.

Today Fellsmere might be more famous for the annual Frog Leg Festival in January, but historians of Indian River County know it as "Birthplace of Equal Suffrage in Florida."

Freaktown, USA
Gibsonton

Half a century ago, people who made their living as sideshow freaks wintered in a small town on the bay just south of Tampa. While walking to the post office or grocery store in Gibsonton, it wasn't unusual to run into a bearded lady, a three-legged man, or a human blockhead famous for hammering ice picks up his nose.

Sideshows are pretty much a thing of the past, but Gibsonton is still home to lots of circus and carnival folk. Many residents of this unpretentious town of 7,000 are ticket takers, clowns, acrobats, animal trainers, and ride mechanics.

The few remaining sideshow stars, who dubbed the place "Freaktown, USA," are reluctant to talk to reporters because of all the negative publicity brought down on Gibsonton by the Lobster Boy case.

Lobster Boy, a.k.a. Grady Stiles Jr., was born with a genetic condition that joined his fingers and toes into two-digit claws. He moved by flopping around on flipperlike legs. Needless to say, he was a sideshow celebrity. Unfortunately, Stiles was also a violent alcoholic. He

★ ★

Giants Camp Restaurant in Gibsonton was once a hangout for circus freaks, including a human "blockhead" famous for hammering ice picks up his nose.

was convicted of killing his daughter's boyfriend, but thanks to testimony from two of his neighbors—a fat man and a bearded lady—he was spared a lengthy prison term.

It was all very unpleasant and embarrassing stuff to the hardworking freaks (a hermaphrodite, an 8-foot-tall man, a woman who walks on glass) of Gibsonton who tried to make an honest living.

Sideshows were done in not so much by political correctness as by medical advances. Better treatments became available for people with physical abnormalities, and pregnant women are now warned against taking certain drugs that can cause deformities.

The weather is still nice in the winter in Gibsonton, but you almost never see a bearded lady on your way to the post office anymore.

Tales from the Crypt

Among the diseases you least want to contract, yellow fever has to rank high on the list.

Symptoms of the mosquito-transmitted disease include chills, fever, headache, vomiting of blood, and bleeding from the gums and nose. The disease gets its name from the fact that some victims become jaundiced and turn yellow. When that happens, there's about a fifty-fifty chance you'll die.

Florida, with its warm climate and abundant lakes and ponds, is very popular with mosquitoes, which could explain why Florida has had so many yellow fever epidemics. The last big one in 1888 killed 400 people in Jacksonville and resulted in the long-overdue creation of the state Board of Health in 1889. By 1918, Florida was yellow fever–free.

Floridians don't think much about the disease now, but back in the early 1800s folks shivered with terror at the mere mention of the words *yellow fever*. It was a terrible disease and about the only good thing that came out of it was a colorful legend.

The story goes that yellow fever victims got so sick that they sometimes appeared dead before they really were. As a result, some victims were buried alive. This was apparently discovered when bodies were disinterred and moved to other cemeteries. Fingernail scratches were sometimes visible inside the coffin lid, and the padding inside was shredded. The "corpse" had obviously been trying to get out.

The solution to this problem involved some trial and error. First, they tried putting some pieces of fried chicken next to the corpse before closing the lid. This was OK in the sense that the victim could enjoy a nice picnic lunch when he woke up, but not OK in the sense that he was still 6 feet underground with no way to get out. (Plus, they often forgot to pack potato salad.)

Next, they tried running an air tube into the coffins. This presumably allowed the victim to breathe, but still gave him no way out.

The final solution involved tying one end of a string to the victim's finger and the other end to a small bell aboveground. The idea was that if the dead person's finger twitched, the bell would ring, and someone would hear it and summon help. The problem was that corpses tended to awake at inconvenient times, when people were away doing other things, like frying chicken or burying people alive. So people were hired to sit by fresh grave sites and listen for the tinkling of the bell. The work was divided into three shifts, the most unpopular being the midnight to 8:00 a.m. stint that came to be called the "graveyard shift."

Two other popular phrases were inspired by this morbid practice. Can you guess what they are?

Dead ringer, and saved by the bell.

Or so the legend goes.

★ ★

Monkeying Around
Homosassa

As a tourist attraction, Monkey Island is not likely to put Disney World out of business anytime soon.

"It's just a bunch of monkeys on an island. What more do you need to know?" That's the way a gentleman at the bar at Charlie Brown's Crab House summed up the situation.

The story's not a great deal more complicated than that. A man by the name of Bruce Norris owned a wildlife attraction up the Homosassa River from the restaurant. When the state purchased the attraction, Norris took some of the ringtail monkeys and relocated them on a little spoil island in the middle of the river, a stone's throw from the restaurant. That was about sixty years ago, and the monkeys, or at least their descendants, remain.

There's a little red-and-white lighthouse on the island, some palm trees, and a tire swing on which the half dozen or so monkeys can cavort. (During our visit, there was precious little cavorting going on, though we did observe some serious languishing.)

Our barroom source told us the monkeys don't swim the few feet to shore because they've got it made on the island, what with daily feedings, the aforementioned tire swing, and a measure, albeit small, of local celebrity.

They were a semi-interesting diversion while we scarfed down a delicious soft-shell crab sandwich at Charlie Brown's, but we expect most folks who visit the river come to watch the manatees, not the monkeys.

After all, it's just a bunch of monkeys on an island. What more do you need to know?

Monkey Island is located right off the dock of Charlie Brown's Crab House in Homosassa Riverside Resort. Take County Road 490 west from Homosassa Springs to Homosassa and follow the signs.

Monument to the Kids
Kissimmee

A trickle of tourists still visits the Monument to the States, amazingly enough, which only proves the durability of even the most mundane tourist attractions. The Kissimmee monument, after all, is merely a tower of stones perched on a corner between the town's main drag and its lakefront park.

For locals, the monument is a relic of the past. During World War II a local booster named Charles Bressler-Pettis came up with the idea of collecting stones from all the states. For neighborhood kids, more than fifty years later, the monument is both a landmark and a dare.

The stone steps of the monument, you see, practically beg to be climbed. Easy handholds crowd all four sides, but there is a devilish overhang near the top of the 50-foot tower. A pair of local basketball players describe the Monument to the States as a Kissimmee rite of passage.

"Kids dare each other to climb to the top," says Michael Merritt. "I made it like halfway and went back down."

Charles Ibbott points more than halfway up. "I got up to the Cape Cod part," he says. "I fell when I got to that red rock."

Considering that this rock is a good 30 feet off the ground, and the fact that Ibbott tells his story with a smile, this is a more dubious claim. Charles Bressler-Pettis, though, would appreciate his sense of promotion.

Spicy and "Spicey" Boiled Peanuts
Lake Hamilton

There's hardly a Panhandle highway, byway, or country lane that doesn't have some lonely soul selling boiled peanuts from a roadside stand. It's usually one person beside a pot filled with boiling nuts ready to be scooped out with a ladle that's sometimes made from a stick and a tin can punched with holes.

Florida
CURIOSITIES

★ ★

Peanuts, the signs say, or P-Nuts. They're often hot peanuts and Cajun peanuts, or spicy and even "spicey" peanuts.

As tourists travel south into the Florida peninsula, boiled peanuts are fewer and farther in between. One of the last outposts is the Nut House, tucked between U.S. Highway 27 and Lake Hamilton west of Orlando and south of Interstate 4.

It's a "spicey" stop, brightly painted, offering quart bags of peanuts for $3. A Confederate flag hangs out back, and chickens cluck in a nearby orange grove as four lanes of traffic rumble by.

Amanda Flowers, a Polk County native working the stand, said the Nut House has been a local favorite since before she was born. Now it's expanding its reach.

"We get people who come all the way here from Orlando and Miami," she said. "They come all the way here, get their peanuts, and turn around and go home. The lady who comes from Miami says there's a stand down there, but she likes ours better."

The Nut House offers green Virginia peanuts that have been soaked for forty-eight hours and boiled for four in a sixty-gallon pot. Regular peanuts are boiled with four cups of salt and a ham hock, while the spicy nuts also get Zatarain's crab boil and crushed red pepper.

Northern tourists often stop at the roadside stand to stretch their legs and satisfy their curiosity.

"They'll come by and never even heard of boiled peanuts," Flowers says. "We tell 'em about them and let 'em taste some."

The Nut House is just north of Lake Hamilton on the west side of US 27.

* *

Swan Lake
Lakeland

There is no record of Richard the Lionhearted ever having visited Lakeland, but his name is connected with this mid-Florida city just the same.

What the two have in common is swans. About 800 years ago,
Richard, who was involved with the Crusades, received a pair of white
mute swans from Queen Beatrice of Cypress. (Today, she would probably have just sent him a bunch of mylar balloons spelling out "Best
of luck!")

Fast forward to 1956. Lakeland, whose ten major lakes had been
home to a varying number of the graceful birds since at least 1923,
saw its last swan fall victim to an alligator in 1954. Mrs. Robert Pick-
hardt, a Lakeland native living in England at the time, was familiar
with the royal flock of swans on the Thames—birds descended from
the original pair given to Richard, he of the lion heart. She inquired
about purchasing a pair for Lakeland. Queen Elizabeth, known to be a
little tight with a farthing, agreed to send a pair of swans to Lakeland
if the city would pay the cost of capture, crating, and shipping, esti-
mated at $300.

Eventually the money was raised, and a pair of white mute swans
from England were released on Lake Morton on February 9, 1957.
Descendants of that pair continue to grace the city's many lakes;
today there are more than 200 birds, including white mutes, Australian black swans, white Coscorba swans from the Falkland Islands,
black-neck swans from South America, white pelicans, ducks, geese,
and other species.

Lakeland has learned its lesson and is very protective of its swans
now. There is an annual swan round-up, at which time the graceful
birds are inoculated against disease, and the city provides feeding stations and breeding pens along Lake Morton's perimeter. An S-necked
swan is now the city's official logo, and a few years ago a swan post-
age stamp was issued out of respect for the bird's place in the city's
history.

A good place to view the swans of Lake Morton is at the corner of Lake Morton Drive and East Palmetto Avenue, near the Lakeland Library. If you're driving, be careful; the swans have the right-of-way.

The Eerie Legend of Spook Hill
Lake Wales

Once upon a time, at a place not far from what is now a convenience store, an Indian town on Lake Wales was plagued by a huge alligator. The town's great warrior chief and the gator were killed in a titanic struggle that created the huge, swampy depression nearby. The chief was buried on the north side of the depression.

Later, pioneer haulers coming from the old Army trail atop the ridge found their horses laboring here, at the foot of the ridge, and called the place Spook Hill.

Is it the gator seeking revenge, or is the chief protecting his land?

Does any of this make any sense to you?

It doesn't make any difference, because the fun of Spook Hill is sitting in your car as it rolls . . . uphill. Or at least that's the way it seems. A sign near the bottom of the hill on North Wales Drive instructs you to stop on the white line and put your car in neutral. Your eyes tell you you're headed downhill, but your car tells you otherwise.

Be sure to check your rearview mirror for cars behind you before you investigate the optical illusion that is Spook Hill; not only do you roll backward, you do so briskly.

Spook Hill is located just down the hill from the intersection of North Wales Drive and Burns Avenue. Small brown signs scattered about town direct you to the place. Right around the corner is Spook Hill Elementary School, the logo for which is, appropriately enough, a ghost. Mind your speed when driving by the school in the morning and afternoon. The tickets the cops hand out are no optical illusion.

* *

Mountain Music
Lake Wales

You won't need Sherpa guides or bottled oxygen to scale the highest "peak" in peninsular Florida.

Located in Lake Wales in Polk County, Iron Mountain tops out at a decidedly nondizzying height of 298 feet above sea level. In other words, it's not quite as high as a football field is long. Forget mountain goats and glaciers; the view from the top is mostly of nondescript orange groves.

In fact, Iron Mountain wouldn't be worthy of mention at all if weren't for Bok's Singing Tower rising from what can laughingly be called its summit. Opened to the public on February 1, 1929, by President Calvin Coolidge, Bok Tower is a 205-foot-high bell tower that houses sixty bronze carillon bells ranging in weight from sixteen pounds to nearly twelve tons. Clock music is played by a mechanical keyboard every half hour beginning at 10:00 a.m. A lengthier recital chimes at 3:00 p.m.

The tower, a gift to the American people from Dutch publisher and author Edward W. Bok, is constructed of pink and gray marble from Georgia and coquina stone (a sort of concrete made with seashells) from St. Augustine. The tower's sculpture and tile work, called faience, depict mostly birds and plants as well as other varieties of wildlife, including seahorses, fish, foxes, tortoises, and, oddly enough, apes.

Surrounded by a moat, the tower is the centerpiece of Bok Tower Gardens, 200 acres of immaculately maintained azaleas, camellias, magnolias, and other flowering trees and plants. A colony of brightly colored wood ducks makes its home in the gardens, as do more than one hundred other wild bird species. The birds are indeed abundant, but the first thing you will notice is the squirrels, which scamper about everywhere and are not the least bit shy about begging for a handout.

The tower, more a work of art than a monument (visitors aren't allowed inside), is a National Historic Landmark, and the gardens are a designated site on the Great Florida Birding Trail. The place is all about beauty and serenity; you'd have to be an uptight person indeed not to feel your cares melt away after spending an hour or two wandering the grounds.

Bok, a Dutch immigrant following the advice of his grandmother, said he wanted to make America more beautiful because he lived in it. Bok Tower Gardens is proof of his success.

Bok Tower Gardens, located at 1151 Tower Boulevard, Lake Wales, is open year-round. Fee. For details call (863) 676-1408.

**One of the most restful places in central Florida.
. . . Just watch out for the squirrels.**

Estate Living

While visiting Bok Tower Gardens, don't forget to tour Pinewood Estate, a twenty-room Mediterranean Revival–style villa on eight acres next to the gardens. Pinewood was called "El Retiro" when it opened in 1929 and was the winter home of C. Austin Buck (not Bok), vice president of Bethlehem Steel. Buck's love of Latin lifestyle and architecture is reflected by his use of Cuban tiles throughout the house and a Spanish frog fountain leading to a grotto in front. Buck hired Frederick Law Olmsted Jr. to design the gardens in keeping with the ecology of Florida. Today, the Pine Ridge Nature Trail, Woodland Garden, and Wildlife Observatory are testimony to that commitment.

Guided tours of Pinewood Estate are offered daily from October through mid-May, at 11:00 a.m. and 1:30 p.m. A six-week special event called Christmas at Pinewood takes place each year beginning the day after Thanksgiving.

Phone (863) 676-1408 or visit www.boktower.org. To get there, take exit 23 from I-4 and drive south on US 27 for about 20 miles. Go past Eagle Ridge Mall for two traffic lights, then turn left on Mountain Lake Cutoff Road and follow the signs. From Tampa and Vero Beach, take State Road 60 to Lake Wales and follow the signs.

Getting the Perfect Tan
Land O' Lakes

With its warm climate and abundant sunshine, Florida is a great place to come to if you want to . . . get naked.

It should come as no surprise that Florida has more nudist resorts and nude beaches than any other state. (Nudists, by the way, refer to

★ ★

vacation spots where clothes are worn as "textile resorts.")

For some reason, the Tampa Bay area is especially thick with nudist resorts. Five of the state's fourteen resorts are located here, including Lake Como Family Nudist Resort in Land O' Lakes, site of the annual Super Bowl South Volleyball Tournament every March.

In business since 1947, Lake Como is the oldest nudist resort in the state. Its clientele is mostly couples and families, and activities include swimming, tennis, volleyball, pentanque (a kind of paddle ball), boating, and, of course, sunning. In the evenings, everyone heads down to the lakeside bar, otherwise known as the "Butt Hutt."

Experienced nudists say that if you're new to the nude-recreation experience, you might want to try a nudist resort before going to a nude beach. (More shade, for one thing.)

For more information on Florida's nudist resorts, call (800) TRY-NUDE (I'm not kidding) or visit the website for the American Association for Nude Recreation at www.aanr.com. (A playful lot, members sometimes like to abbreviate their organization's name to American Ass. for Nude Recreation.)

But if you do decide to visit one of Florida's nudist resorts, remember one thing: Bring lots of sunscreen.

Peacocks in Paradise
Longboat Key

Longboat Key is a cloistered island community known for its pricey condominiums, gorgeous sunsets and . . . peacocks?

If you want to start an argument, just walk around the northeastern part of the Key known as the Village and proclaim your love/hatred of the approximately 60 peacocks that—literally—dot the community.

The anti-peacock faction claims that the birds devour their gardens, poop on their pool cages and emit a terrifying shriek that sounds (we're guessing) like a baby being stabbed.

The defenders of the peacocks tend to be people like Pat

The peacocks of Longboat Key have ruffled some residents' feathers.

Herrmann who believe that the non-native birds are simply a part of nature that should be accommodated by people.

"People need to learn to live with things," said Herrmann, who proudly recalls the time when forty peacocks perched on her roof.

Herrmann claims the peacocks have become a tourist attraction, which probably rankles privacy-minded Longboat residents more than the peacocks themselves.

A quick drive around the Village on a cold January morning revealed about a half-dozen peacocks (or peafowl, if you want to be technical) strutting across the street, perching on rooftops and just generally flaunting their gaudy plumage in the bright winter sunshine.

★ ★

None seemed concerned one way or the other about the controversy roiling all around them but all seemed eager to pose for the camera.

If Longboat Key officials have their way, there will soon be fewer of the colorful (and rapidly reproducing) peacocks to photograph. The plan is to relocate all but about a dozen birds to rural areas where pool cages are in short supply and peacock poop is looked upon as free fertilizer.

The relocation efforts are likely to lead to another battle in the Peacock Wars unless some other threat takes precedence like, maybe, squirrels.

Wait a Cotton Pickin' Minute
Longboat Key

The World's Tallest Cotton Plant is, quite frankly, not much to look at. Think of a grapevine as thick as a man's arm twisting upward 30 feet, 4 inches (as of the last measure in November, 2009). There are a few brownish-green leaves, some yellow flowers (yes, cotton plants have flowers) and here and there a few tufts of fluffy white cotton.

But what makes the cotton plant amazing besides its stupendous height (it, and its somewhat less tall cousins, have been listed in the *Guinness Book of World Records* several times), is its location. It grows in the sandy, salty, and extremely high-priced soil of Longboat Key, a tony barrier island on Florida's southwest coast. You expect to see sea grape there, or palm trees or maybe a hibiscus or two. But not cotton.

The cotton plant is the labor of love of D. M. Williams, a seventy-seven-year-old former cotton picker from West Texas. Williams is the manager of Casa del Mar beach resort at 4621 Gulf of Mexico Drive. When Williams left Texas, he swore he never wanted to see another cotton plant as long as he lived. But a brother (he's one of eleven kids) convinced him otherwise. He brought Williams some seeds that had been crossed with rare green and brown cotton plants. He thinks it's the crossbreeding that resulted in a cotton plant of fairy-tale proportion.

"That and a lot of chicken (poop)," he said, laughing.

The 30-foot-plus plant is Williams' tallest so far, and it sprouted by accident. A seed from an earlier plant blew over next to the resort's maintenance shed and sprouted. Williams and assistant manager Mark Meador attached guy wires to the monster to keep it from falling over in high winds; they spray the salt off of it and put propane heaters under it when the temperature drops below 30, which it seldom does in these parts. And, of course, they fertilize it.

Williams, a garrulous fellow, welcomes sightseers (people from as far away as Iceland have stopped by) and he'll be glad to tell you everything you might want to know about what it's like to live in tall cotton. (Hey, you thought we were going to get all the way through this without using that line?)

Contact Williams at Casa del Mar, Longboat Key, Florida. The phone number is (941) 383-1716. The website is www.casadelmar.net.

Space Coast Countdown
Melbourne

In 1998, when it was time for a new telephone area code in central Florida, a man named Robert "Ozzie" Osband had a singular idea. The Titusville programmer and consultant—he calls himself a "computerist"—thought he had the perfect new area code for Brevard County, Cape Canaveral, and what's known as "The Space Coast."

3–2–1.

Get it? 3–2–1, as in blast off.

Osband's idea for the area code was an immediate hit. Governor Jeb Bush called it "a brilliant idea" at a National Space Club dinner, and the number was adopted by the Florida Public Service Commission. In 1999, the change even appeared as a final question on *Jeopardy:* "In 1999, several counties around Cape Canaveral, Florida, were assigned this new telephone area code." The correct answer, of course, was "What is 3-2-1?"

On his Spacey Ideas website, Osband crowed that "321 is MY area code! (But I share.) I asked for it, they approved, so it's mine, right?"

He also published *Via Oz,* a fanzine explaining the development of the area code. At a computer conference, under the hacker identity of "The Cheshire Catalyst," he gave a talk called "How I Got My Own Area Code."

Last, but not least, or at least for a brief while, Osband snagged the coolest phone number in the area: (321) LIFTOFF.

Costume Cowboys
Miakka

South of Tampa, it's the Miakka Misfits. North of Tampa, the Doodle Hill Regulators. In Orlando, there's the Weewahootee Vigilance Committee. Not to mention the Cowford Regulators, Withlacoochee Renegades, and the Lake County Pistoleros.

Throughout Florida, men and women enjoy the sport of Cowboy Action Shooting.

They dress up in the wildest of Wild West costumes. Big hats. Long coats. Lots of holsters and bandoliers. Newcomers are advised to dress like characters in a B-grade Western, with appropriately colorful aliases. "Hungry Bear" and "Salsa Sure Shot." "Hoss McCabe" and "Jeremiah Longknife." "Burt Blade" and "Arcadia Butcher."

Shooters meet at gun ranges to fire real weapons at steel targets. In a typical round, the shooter stands at a mock stockade, grabs his shotgun, and fires at two targets. Then he trots to another spot and fires five rifle shots. Then he hustles to a third station and fires six to eight shots with his pistols. For every target missed, five seconds is added to his time. If a shooter hits each and every target, he gets a special cheer from the crowd.

"Can I get a yee-ha?" somebody shouts. Everyone yells back, "Yee-ha!"

Tim "Deadlee" Headlee, president of the Miakka Misfits, owns a gas station in real life. He said the group's monthly outings are nothing like precision shooting, which tends to be serious and competitive.

Steve Solomon dresses up as "Cracker Jake" for Cowboy Action Shooting with the Miakka Misfits and the Doodle Hill Regulators.

Action shooting is more like a pastime. "The targets are big and close," Headlee said, "and you get to run around and basically play cowboy like when you were a kid, only with real guns."

Safety rules are strict. No one walks around with a loaded weapon. Before a round, shooters load their guns at one table. After a round, they unload their guns at another table.

Steve Solomon, a Bradenton construction manager, shoots with the Misfits and the Doodle Hill Regulators. He dresses up as "Cracker Jake," with a bright blue shirt and broad-brimmed hat. Garters hold up his sleeves, and leather wrist guards cover his cuffs. A salt-and-pepper goatee completes the look.

★ ★

Solomon already had shooting experience before he took up the sport, but had forgotten how to play cowboy. "The transition is the biggest learning curve, learning to transition from gun to gun," Solomon said. "My pistols—I'm always trying to push too fast with them. The faster you try to go, the slower you go."

Albert Burstein, a shooter from Sarasota, wears a modest gray ensemble. He chose the alias "Blackhawk" from the name of a gun manufacturer. In real life, Burstein has a Ph.D. in engineering and designs artificial joints. He's nationally known in his field, but that doesn't mean much in the Miakka Misfits, which is fine by him. "Nobody talks about what they do," he said. "It's an equal playing field for everybody."

Burstein says Cowboy Action Shooting is more relaxed and less competitive than the skeet shooting he used to do. It's more like a colorful hobby he can enjoy with his wife, "Miss Myra" Burstein. They've come a long way from Brooklyn, where they didn't shoot with a posse.

"Now we're starting to watch the old cowboy movies," Burstein said, laughing. "We watch them from a different perspective."

For more information on Cowboy Action Shooting, visit the Single Action Shooting Society at www.sassnet.com or call (941) 650-8920.

Rock of Ages
Mulberry

The Mulberry Phosphate Museum may well be the world's only museum dedicated to . . . fertilizer.

The galleries, some of which are inside a train caboose, tell the story of phosphate, a gray rock mined extensively in and around Mulberry in a section of the state known as Bone Valley. The name comes from the fact that the phosphate rock, formed millions of years ago when Florida was underwater, is intermingled with Cenozoic-era fossils. The fossilized bones of mastodons, saber-toothed tigers, rhinos, and boxcar-length prehistoric sharks are on display in another part of the little museum.

★ ★

The Mulberry Phosphate Museum may be the world's only museum devoted to fertilizer.

The phosphate rock is gouged out of the ground with giant drag-lines, the buckets on which are the size of a small house and can remove 70,000 pounds of material in a single scoop. The museum has a dragline bucket on the grounds. You can stand inside it and have your picture taken. Drive less than a mile east of town on State Road 60 and you can see for yourself what phosphate mining does to the countryside. (Think moonscape.)

The self-guided museum tour briefly addresses the problems associated with phosphate mining, including water pollution and habitat destruction, but because the museum is by, for, and of the phosphate industry, the displays mostly concentrate on the positive aspects of phosphate.

Indeed, phosphate is an important ingredient in fertilizer and animal feed. Many household items contain phosphate, or a derivative of phosphate, including Crest toothpaste, Purina Puppy Chow, and Slim-Fast. And that tingle you get when you take a swig of Coca-Cola? Phosphoric acid. (And all this time you thought it was a sugar high.)

The fact that you might be brushing your teeth with ten-million-year-old crab poop could be disconcerting to some, which is why the phosphate industry would rather you think of the stuff in terms of bountiful harvests and an answer to world hunger.

(Also, it is not true that the phosphate museum's video presentation lasts ten million years. It just seems that long.)

The Mulberry Phosphate Museum is located at 101 S.E. First Street, at the corner of State Road 37 in Mulberry. The museum is open Tuesday through Saturday from 10:00 a.m. to 4:30 p.m. Admission is free, but donations are accepted. Phone (863) 425-2823.

Grape Expectations
Myakka City

Nestled amid the orange groves, cattle ranches, and tomato fields of eastern Manatee County, the Rosa Fiorelli Winery is about as far from Napa Valley as you can get, both geographically and psychologically.

The fact that wine is made at all in Florida is an oddity; the fact that the Fiorelli wines taste pretty darned good is nothing short of astonishing. The owners, Antonio Fiorelli and his wife, Rosa, both natives of Sicily, have succeeded in confounding the conventional wisdom that central Florida's heat, humidity, and sandy soil would make such a thing impossible.

The grapes are harvested from the ten-acre vineyard in June; the wine making takes place in a garage-size building on the grounds. In Florida, as it is everywhere, wine making is a lot of work.

"You've got to constantly check the grapes for insects, mold, mildew, everything," says Antonio. "If you think all there is to it is sticking a grapevine in the ground and walking away, you won't make it."

With some award-winning wines to his credit and public awareness of this most unusual of Florida crops increasing, Antonio Fiorelli figures to be one of the ones who will make it. The fact that he named his winery after his wife didn't hurt either.

The Rosa Fiorelli Winery is located at 4020 County Road 675. For more information, call (914) 322-0976 or visit the website at www.fiorelliwinery.com.

The Big Puddle
Okeechobee

The biggest curiosity in Florida could be Lake Okeechobee, which means "Big Water" in the Seminole language. The lake covers more than 700 square miles, and is easily visible from space, but never gets more than 15 feet deep. So it's basically a big puddle that drains into the Everglades—or used to, before man ruined the natural plumbing of South Florida.

The lake may be big, but most people drive around it without ever seeing water. That's because the Okeechobee is surrounded by the Herbert Hoover Dike, built after a 1928 hurricane flooded the area and killed 2,000 people. This massive levee is 30 feet tall—twice as high as the lake is deep—and 130 miles long.

Parts of the dike are lined with the Lake Okeechobee Scenic Trail, the acronym for which happens to be "LOST." Long-distance cyclists rave about pedaling around the lake for a unique perspective on endless water and limitless sky. Wildlife along the way includes a great variety of wading birds, along with gators of all sizes. Hope Clough, a retired nurse in the town of Okeechobee who pedals a short portion of the scenic trail, has a reptilian favorite. "There's a 15-foot alligator

★ ★

Lots of Florida cyclists enjoy the 13-mile bike trail atop the Herbert Hoover Dike that surrounds Lake Okeechobee.

along the levee, by those trailers," she said. "We named him Fred."

The *Weekly World News,* which is unreliable even by tabloid standards, has reported that there is a "Lake Okeechobee Monster" more terrifying than the famous creature of Loch Ness. It is possible, though, that this publication exaggerated or even fabricated monstrous claims in order to entertain its supermarket readers. Call it a hunch.

Lake Okeechobee, on the other hand, is very shallow but very real. You just have to pedal up to look down at it.

Somewhere, over the Swampy Bog
Ona

From the swamps of Hardee County rises Solomon's Castle, one man's rural image of Oz. Naturally, there's a yellow brick road leading up to the place, which belongs to Howard Solomon, part tinkerer, part artist, and 100 percent a hoot.

Variously called the Da Vinci of Debris or Rembrandt of Reclamation, Solomon has created a 12,000-square-foot museum/home/castle/restaurant/gallery that invariably leaves visitors scratching their heads. The "shingles" of the castle are aluminum offset printing plates discarded by the *Herald-Advocate* newspaper in nearby Wauchula. The turrets sparkle with stained-glass windows made by Solomon, and at the entrance are two armored statues, one white, the other black, called *Day* and *Knight.*

Funny wordplay, you will quickly discover, is as big a part of the Solomon's Castle experience as the 200 pieces of "found art." Solomon does not just conduct a tour; he gives a performance. He steers visitors past an animal menagerie made of fifty pounds of coat hangers, then on to a motorcycle made from an old corn planter, nicknamed "Evil Corn-Evil." Keep your eye open for the goblin under the living room floor and the kitchen elevator that runs on a car battery.

All of the art is made from junk either found by Solomon or donated to him. There are cars and chairs made of beer cans, a lion made of five oil drums cut into pieces, and a gun collection. One gun, made of half a hacksaw and a jack, is called "Hacked-Off Jacksaw." Alongside is a pair of dueling pistols with their barrels bent backward. Solomon claims, with a straight face, that they belonged to the Rev. Jim Jones.

A high-school dropout, Solomon became proficient in more than twenty trades, including welding, shipbuilding, carpentry, and plumbing. While other more conventional artists might have paint and brushes in their studios, Solomon's is filled with welders, steel saws, wood saws, grinders, sandblasters, and shears. Some of the machines Solomon made himself as a teenager.

★ ★

A native of Rochester, New York, Solomon moved to Florida when he was twenty-one. He bought fifty-five acres of land in rural Hardee County, not knowing that the property became a swamp in the summer. But that wasn't much of a problem for the resourceful Solomon. He built levees and installed pumps to drain the land. Perhaps to remind himself of his mistake, Solomon dug a moat around his castle and built the Boat on the Moat restaurant, fashioned after a Spanish galleon.

Solomon's Castle is open for lunch from 11:00 a.m. to 4:00 p.m. Tuesday through Sunday, and for dinner on Saturday from 6:00 to 11:00 p.m. The castle is closed on Monday and throughout July, August and September. Admission is charged. For information, call (863) 494-6077.

From Bradenton, drive east on State Road 64, 28 miles past the Interstate 75 overpass. Turn right on County Road 665 and drive 9 more miles. Solomon Road will be on your left.

Wakeboarding to Music
Orlando

At the Orlando Watersports Complex, where a cable system pulls wakeboarders around a man-made lake, thrill seekers skim, skip, and flip across a variety of rails, slides, and ramps. They don't need a boat. All they need is a board, the cost of admission, and the nerve to sling-shot across the water.

"You come full speed into it and you just launch," said wakeboarder Cory Reiter. "You go crazy high and, especially on this cable, with the turns and with the speed that it brings you, it just brings you up in the air straight. You can do pretty much anything you want while in the air. You can do flips, you can do spins, you can grab the board, grab whatever you want."

It's a teen scene at the OWC, with boys in board shorts and girls in bikinis. A sound system plays alternative rock, but not too loudly, so the grown-ups don't complain.

For young wakeboarders, the park is an escape from the tyranny of boating supervision. They're free to grab a cheap board, or rent a better one, and carve a wake on their own. Older kids gather on Saturday nights, when the park stays open until midnight. Orlando disc jockeys provide the music.

There's a beginner area at the Orlando park, too. No ramps, no rails. The cables are slower and more forgiving. Still, lots of newcomers get dunked, especially jumping off the dock. Grabbing a tow rope and skimming across the water is a lot like leaving a ski lift and heading downhill at a mountain resort.

Reiter said there's nothing like trying your first jump. "These aren't scary, the little ones, but when you get up to that big one, you get up to it, and you turn away, you get up to it, and you turn away, about ten times. After a few times looking at it, you size it up, you go up, and once you do it, it's an accomplishment. Each one of these is an accomplishment, definitely an accomplishment."

The Orlando Watersports Complex, 8615 Florida Rock Road, is in an industrial complex just south of State Road 528, the Beachline Expressway. Take exit 8, then turn right on Jetport, left on Landspeed, and follow the OWC billboard. Admission is charged by the hour, or you can purchase an all-day pass.

For details visit www.orlandowatersports.com or call (407) 251-3100.

World's Largest McDonald's
Orlando

Orlando wouldn't be Orlando—a mind-boggling expanse of tourism great and small, bright and loud, tacky and tackier—without the World's Largest McDonald's and PlayPlace. If Mickey D's wasn't there, to paraphrase Voltaire's famous quip about God, it would have been necessary to invent it.

It fits Orlando like the ears on that other Mickey's head.

This McDonald's claims to be the largest, but so do a few others.

★ ★

This McDonald's is busy, located between I-4 and International Drive, but franchises in Moscow and Beijing have more customers. No, it's not size or scale that makes this "the most unique McDonald's in the world." In a fast-food chain that prizes conformity above all else—a french fry in Tampa must taste exactly like a french fry in Tacoma— this Mickey D's is downright strange, even by Orlando standards.

Along with the three-story jungle gym and video game arcade, there is a pizza counter and ice-cream parlor (both closed on a recent visit). There is a small alligator tank, courtesy of Gatorland (empty on a recent visit). There is a waterfall, plus a souvenir stand and a birth-day party area with a throne set next to a Ronald McDonald statue.

A page one *Orlando Sentinel* story from August 16, 1992, is framed on the wall. The headline: "McEverything but the McKitchen Sink."

In the Maui room, decorated with a Hawaiian motif, a small plaque hidden behind a garbage can explains the personality behind the place. It seems that owners Gary and Jeanie Oerther were married on the island, and it's their favorite place in the world—after Orlando. The golden-arched signs in the parking lot, instead of saying Wel-come, offer Aloha.

Besides all the food and entertainment, the place offers life les-sons, including "Ronald's Way to Play":

- Be a friend! Take turns and share. Big kids, help the little kids and have fun!
- Leave toys, food, and other stuff back at the tables.
- Play safe! Enter the play area slowly, so you don't bump into anybody.
- Leave your shoes here!
- Kids 3 to 12 can play. Parents, too!

Those parents may or may not enjoy Mickey D's, but kids take to the place the way fries take to ketchup. They're scarfing down food, clambering through the jungle gym, and pouring tokens into the video games.

For many, it looks like a visit to Orlando wouldn't be a visit to Orlando without a stop at the World's Largest McDonald's.

Mickey D's is at 6875 Sandlake Road, exit 29 off I–4. Call (407) 351-2185 for more information.

World's Largest Strawberry
Plant City

OK, it's not really a strawberry; it's just a painting of one, atop the water tower in Plant City. But if there were an official world's largest strawberry, you'd probably find it here, in the self-described "Winter Strawberry Capital of the World."

Plant City, in eastern Hillsborough County, is to strawberries what Indian River is to oranges and Apalachicola is to oysters. Twenty percent of America's strawberries come from Florida, and a good portion of those are grown in Hillsborough County. When most people think of Hillsborough County, they think of the big city of Tampa. Few know that Hillsborough has 2,600 fruit and vegetable farms, an annual agricultural output worth $400 million.

Plant City hosts an annual strawberry festival that dates back to 1930. Held in late February and early March, the festival features a strawberry shortcake eating contest, a strawberry picking contest, and, of course, the crowning of Miss Strawberry. While some may come for the swine and steer judging, most come to gorge on strawberries, with or without shortcake.

Quick strawberry trivia question: How do you know that you have no life? Answer: When your idea of a good time is counting the number of seeds on a strawberry. We'll save you the trouble; the average number is 200.

Plant City is not, as you might expect, named after the pervasive strawberry plant. It's named after Henry Plant, a bigshot Florida railroad tycoon who fixed the little town up with its first set of tracks back in 1885. The town was called Hichipuckassa at the time, but citizens wisely decided to rename the town after its benefactor. A

Hichipuckassa Strawberry Festival just wouldn't have the same ring to it.

For information on the festival, log on to www.flstrawberryfestival .com or phone (813) 752-9194.

DQU, and the U Is for Urinal
Port Charlotte

Turn off I-75 at exit 170, stop at the BP gas station and walk into the ladies room at the Dairy Queen. There you will find what has been voted one of the five most fascinating urinals in the world.

Joining the ranks of the facilities at the New York Marathon, London's Millennium Dome, the public restroom at Rothesay in Scotland, and the Kowloon Sheraton Hotel in Hong Kong is the women's urinal here in Port Charlotte.

It might make you lose your appetite, but it will pique your curiosity. If you ask the DQ clerks what the heck the sign means, they'll sigh and point to the ladies' restroom. Go to that restroom, knock loudly to make sure no one is inside, and you'll get your first glimpse of what the French might call *un pissoir pour les femmes.*

Yes, indeed, it's a urinal for women. A "she-inal," if you will, that allows women to urinate while standing up. It is perhaps one of a kind, and that's the reason it attracted the interest of a certain website that ranked it fourth among the world's urinals.

Besides gaining recognition on Urinal.net, the "she-inal" has gotten attention from local newspapers and far-off radio stations. Journalists contact store owner Jim Coulter, who welcomes the attention. The "she-inal" was developed about ten years ago by a Pensacola woman named Kathie Jones. It was marketed by a company called Urinette, which is no longer in business. Coulter believes a previous owner installed the device in an attempt to get around adding facilities for the handicapped.

Those interested in trying out the she-inal will have to go home disappointed. A sign next to the device reads, "This is only for amusement purposes. Please do not use."

Twistee Treat's Swirly Shops
Port Charlotte

Way back in the 1980s, when Florida boomed and snowbirds flocked to the state, Twistee Treat served soft ice cream up and down the Gulf Coast. The North Fort Myers snack chain didn't need signs—its tiny shops were shaped like swirly ice cream cones, complete with a cherry on top.

An old Twistee Treat building welcomes visitors to the KidStar Amusement Park in Port Charlotte.

★ ★

Things have changed since then.

The Florida boom went bust—as did Twistee Treat—which left a string of empty buildings shaped like ice cream cones. Now the 28-foot-tall fiberglass buildings are being sold, moved and recycled all over the country.

Some look old and faded. A few have been repainted to look like strawberry cones. In some cases, the old vanilla cone got a realistic drip of chocolate syrup.

There are Internet websites, naturally, that track these businesses. Many are still Twistee Treat. Others are called The Cone, King Cone and Chubby's Treats. One shop in Niagara Falls, New York, draws customers as the Twist o' the Mist. In Port Charlotte, a Twistee Treat cone has been turned into an entrance and concession stand for the Kidstar Amusement Park just off the Tamiami Trail. Parents who bring their kids to birthday parties get a kick out of this creamy blast from the past.

"People ask where to buy tickets," said Steve Sherwood, who works at the park. "We say, 'Go to the ice cream building.'"

Tracking an Eight-Track Tape Collector
Port Charlotte

Once upon a time, before Madonna and MTV, before compact discs and MP3s, there was a commercial recording format known as eight-track tape. The big, clunky tapes came along in the late 1960s and allowed people to listen to their favorite music in their cars. At the time, this was a very big deal. Soon, of course, there were audiocassettes, and then digital music formats, and eight-track went the way of the dodo bird.

Except, of course, for "trackers" such as Stephen Pearl of Port Charlotte.

He prefers the hiss and hum of old tapes to the cold quiet of the most modern technology. From a workshop in his small apartment, he collects eight-track tapes—pre-Beatles rock and roll, mostly—and repairs eight-track players.

**Eight-tracks are making a comeback among collectors
who like tape untangling as much as they like music.**

"It's good therapy for me, and I hate to see people throw eight-tracks away when they're still good," Pearl says. "I don't charge people hardly anything because I'm not really doing it for the money."

For eight-track fans, there's a whole subculture devoted to the medium. A website, www.8trackheaven.com, promises to be "digital online, but analog at heart." A documentary, *So Right They're Wrong,* followed fans underground, where they read a quarterly magazine, *8-Track Mind,* and follow Eight Noble Truths.

These include "Naive is not a dirty word," "New and improved don't necessarily mean the same thing," and "State of the art is in the eye of the beholder."

★ ★

Pearl might be proof of that. He's got CD players and everything else, but enjoys an afternoon spent cracking open plastic boxes and splicing tape. He's a former security guard with bifocals and a graying beard, and has plenty of time to devote to his hobby.

"When you go to digital, I think you lose a lot," he says. "Everything's perfect, and the original recordings were never perfect. Personally, I don't think anything modern sounds as good."

Swimming for Freedom
Punta Gorda

Charlotte County's annual Freedom Swim, a Fourth of July tradition for more than a decade, draws all sorts of people to the Peace River. Some people actually swim more than a mile from Port Charlotte to Punta Gorda. Some people swim a little bit, kick a little bit, and float a little bit. Some people float with foam noodles. Some people float with inflatable tubes. And some people float with makeshift rafts carrying cold beverages, silly signs, and the occasional dog wearing a red-white-and-blue bandanna.

The few hard-core swimmers always get swamped by hundreds of easygoing floaters.

Mike Haymans, one of the Charlotte founders, describes the Freedom Swim as more of a "happening" than a race. There are no trophies, medals, or official times. And there's always been more skinny-dipping than sprinting. The tea-colored water of the Peace River keeps this practice from being too naughty.

Organizers recommend the buddy system for participants who swim at their own risk. The marine patrol and volunteer boaters try to keep an eye on stragglers. Smart swimmers wear sunscreen and drink lots of water or sports drinks, to keep from getting dehydrated in the middle of the river. The fastest swimmers cross the Peace River in less than an hour. The founders bring up the rear in three hours or more. The race is set for a time when an ebb tide will help pull people along and across.

★ ★

Hundreds of swimmers and paddlers cross the Peace River each Fourth of July in the annual Freedom Swim.

Newcomers may fear alligators or sharks, but old-timers worry more about cutting their feet on shells along the river bottom. The Peace River is shallow enough that swimmers can walk for a hundred yards or more at the start of the Freedom Swim.

During the event, the water's crowded with people, canoes, kayaks, personal watercraft, and powerboats. Spectators line the Gilchrist Bridge and cheer the start and the swimmers. The Freedom Swim seems to grow each July, but it remains blissfully disorganized. No one's ever printed up T-shirts, for instance, though there would seem to be all sorts of appropriate slogans.

"I Survived the Freedom Swim." Nah, too predictable. "I Burned My Butt at the Freedom Swim and All I Got Was This Lousy T-Shirt." Too wordy. "Skinny-dipping for Freedom." Now that one's not bad.

And it would give the dippers something to wear when they climb out of the water. For details call (941) 639-7002.

A Ninety-Nine-Year-Old Snake Charmer
Punta Gorda

Even at the age of ninety-nine, closing in on an astonishing century of risk and adventure, Bill Haast still tangles with cobras. Every morning the Punta Gorda man collects venom from hissing and lunging cobras, along with vipers, rattlesnakes, and coral snakes. He pulls them from cages, coming within inches of their fangs before seizing them behind the head with swift, sure hands.

The New Jersey native, a flight engineer during World War II, injects himself with venom every other day. The idea is to build up his immunity in case of accidental bites from poisonous snakes. He's survived some 169 bites, a mark recognized by the *Guinness Book of World Records,* so he must be doing something right.

Medical researchers use Haast's freeze-dried venom, but he made his fame and fortune with an old Florida tourist attraction called the Miami Serpentarium. Even today, when safer methods are available, he's happy to demonstrate snake-handling skills for the film crews who make pilgrimages to his Gulf Coast laboratory.

For more than a decade, Bill and Nancy Haast have lived and worked along Shell Creek in eastern Charlotte County. She's his wife, lab assistant, press liaison, office manager, and friendly voice on the phone. They're busy every day, caring for the laboratory, grounds, and more than 1,000 poisonous snakes.

"You know, our lives, we're pretty focused," Nancy says, laughing. "We're not like most people."

For many snake handlers in Florida, Haast is a still-living legend. Bruce Dangerfield, a Vero Beach animal control officer, helps supply

You're over ninety, you're living in paradise, you're . . . handling snakes?!?

Haast with poisonous snakes, bringing along friends to visit the spry old man in Punta Gorda. "He's my hero, without a doubt," Danger-field says. "It's just amazing to see the things he does. He's bouncing around like a kid, and he's sharp as a tack. I'll tell you what, he's the most fantastic person I've ever met."

Critics call Haast an exhibitionist, someone who takes need-less risks, but Dangerfield finds that part of the old man's charm. "He's probably a little safer when he's by himself; I'm sure Nancy sees to that," he says. "He's still a showman—not a showoff, but a showman."

Just about every day, Haast wears white—white shirt, white belt, white pants—a practice that dates back to his shows at the Serpentarium. He's got a shock of white hair that Nancy trims for him, because he won't bother going to town for a haircut. When *Outside* magazine did an interview with him in 1996, the photo was dramatically lit, making Haast look like the mad scientist in an old black-and-white movie.

In person, though, Haast has an easy laugh and strong memory for names, dates, and places. He's short and trim, about as fit as a ninety-nine-year-old man can be. Except for his hands: They're still quick enough to catch cobras, but his fingers are crabbed and swollen from the bites he's gotten over the years. He's missing his right pinkie from a cottonmouth bite.

Both Haasts would like their venom collection business to continue after they're gone. Nancy has a list of apprentices who could help with the snake handling if something happened to Bill. Haast remains healthy enough to laugh at the idea.

"If I go before Nancy, we've got no problem," he says, flashing a big smile. "If she goes before me, then we've got a problem. I can't even work the computer." The Haast laboratory is not open to the public, but there are occasional group tours. For more information, call (941) 639-8888.

Whimsy Land
Safety Harbor

Artists Todd Ramquist and Kiaralinda—just Kiaralinda—moved north of St. Petersburg in the 1980s. They bought a house on Third Street in Safety Harbor. It was beige.

It's not beige anymore.

Now Whimsy, as they call their studio home, features teal walls, purple accents, and red and yellow windows. Colorful painted tiles trim the windows and doorways. Colorful painted buoys hang from the roofline. And colorful painted bowling balls—hundreds of them—line paths through the yard.

The place draws double takes from visitors to the neighborhood.

"People have become accustomed to walking around the yard," Ramquist said. "We just keep working and let them wander around."

Fortunately, the "Whimsy Twinz," as they call themselves, aren't shy. The far-out place fits their personalities. Their studio has been shown on *Oprah* and featured on *Roadside Attractions* on PBS. In 2000 the pair decorated a Volkswagen Beetle as "Tooky, the Y2K Bug." In 2001 they wrote a book called *On the Ball.* In 2005 they used hundreds of colorful beads and tiles to decorate "Whimzee the Manatee." For years they recruited neighbors to create over-the-top Christmas installations.

Now the artists don't live so much in Safety Harbor. They love to travel. And they spend their summers outside of Chicago in a tiki-style home with a Hawaiian theme. Of course.

For more information visit www.kiaralinda.com or call (727) 725-4018.

Big Airboats and Giant Gators

Sarasota

In South Florida, between Miami and Naples, dozens of little airboats take small groups of tourists on gator-spotting tours of the Everglades. On the Gulf Coast, between Tampa and Fort Myers, two giant airboats take large groups of visitors to see the huge alligators of Myakka River State Park.

The *Gator Gal* and *Myakka Maiden* are 50 feet long, and carry more than seventy passengers, but they only draw about a foot of water. That means they can glide right up to the sand banks of Upper Lake Myakka.

Often there are dozens of gators—big gators, some 12 and 14 feet long. Sometimes they rest on the beach with their mouths gaping open, revealing pink gullets and long rows of white teeth. This is when dozens of tourists snap hundreds of photographs.

★ ★

Airboat captains double as tour guides. They often spot wading birds, osprey and even bald eagles, but gators are the main attraction. The guides explain how the temperature of a gator nest determines the sex of the eggs that hatch into baby gators. When the warmth of a nest exceeds 90 degrees, the gators are male.

During an hour-long tour, every visitor learns, or re-learns, the rule of thumb for judging the size of an alligator. Every inch from the eye to the nostril equals a foot in overall length. In other words, an 8-inch snout equals an 8-foot gator.

The *Gator Gal* and *Myakka Maiden* are much bigger, which is a comfort for worried tourists. The captains like to say that these tour vessels are the biggest airboats in the world. They've never heard of any bigger, anyway.

Myakka River State Park is 9 miles east of Sarasota on State Road 72, exit 205 on Interstate 75. The park is open every day from 8:00 a.m. to sunset. Admission is $6 per vehicle. Airboat tours are $12 per person, $6 for kids.

For more information, visit www.myakkariver.org or call (941) 361-6511.

Tourist Attractions, B.D. (Before Disney)
Sarasota

If it's long lines, high prices, and stomach-churning roller coasters you're looking for, then Sarasota Jungle Gardens is not the place for you.

One of Florida's oldest tourist attractions, Jungle Gardens was a swampy banana grove in the early 1930s when Sarasota newspaperman David Lindsay bought the ten-acre tract with the idea of turning the virgin subtropical jungle into a botanical garden.

Lindsay and his partner, Pearson Conrad, brought in thousands of tropical plants, trees, and flowers from all over the world. Artesian well–fed streams and a central lake give the place the feel of a leafy oasis just a few blocks from busy U.S. Highway 41.

Opened in December 1940 as a tourist attraction, Sarasota Jungle

★ ★

Forget roller coasters and fireworks—flamingos are the centerpiece of Sarasota's Jungle Gardens, one of Florida's oldest tourist attractions.

Gardens has changed little over the years, which adds considerably to its unique charm. As you begin walking the trail beneath a canopy of Australian nut trees, bunya-bunya trees, strangler figs, and royal palms, you feel as if you are alone in the place. Abundant benches encourage the visitor to pause and enjoy the tranquility, or maybe engage the resident kookaburra or spider monkey in conversation.

Probably the favorite place to pause in Jungle Gardens is Flamingo Lagoon, where black swans, white swans, and, of course, flamingos make you wish you had brought along more color film. (The good folks in the gift shop will be happy to fix you up.)

But even a low-key tourist attraction needs a spectacle of some sort, and at Jungle Gardens, the *Birds of the Rainforest* show is

★ ★

unquestionably the main event. Have you ever seen a bird roller-skate, balance atop a basketball, or ride a bicycle on a high wire? Trained macaws and cockatoos do these things and more.

Frosty, a greater sulfur-crested cockatoo, is about seventy years old and has been doing his act at Jungle Gardens since 1972. Frosty appeared on the *Ed Sullivan Show*; others, like Paulette, a blue-and-gold macaw, have starred in commercials.

Believe it or not, the birds were trained by inmates at Chino State Prison in California as part of a prisoner enrichment program designed to teach sensitivity and respect. (If the birds learned any rough language while in prison, they have the good manners to keep it to themselves.) Don't forget to visit the reptile exhibit, which contains live specimens of every American poisonous snake except the coral snake, which does not fare well in captivity. The main attraction here is a 14-foot African rock python that was found slithering about in the woods about 10 miles east of Jungle Gardens near I-75. The 200-pound snake was apparently somebody's pet that escaped.

No word yet on whether the prisoners at Chino have any interest in teaching this fella how to ride a bicycle on a high wire.

Sarasota Jungle Gardens, located at 3701 Bay Shore Road, is open every day except Christmas from 9:00 a.m. to 5:00 p.m. Admission is charged; annual passes are available. For more information call (941) 355-5305 or visit the website www.sarasotajunglegardens.com.

TAC the Knife
Sarasota

Meet Tom Johanning, maker of the TAC-11, the knife preferred by Rambos the world over.

Johanning is a machinist and owner of the prosaically named Florida Knife Company. You've probably never heard of him unless you're a Navy SEAL, a SEAL wannabe, or the kind of person who wants a knife that can hack off a tree limb or pry open a car door and still remain sharp enough to shave the hairs off your arm.

The TAC in the name is short for "tactical," and the 11 means it's 11 inches long. This is not the kind of knife you whittle sticks with while rocking on the front porch.

Only you can tell you why you need a TAC-11, but we can tell you how it's made. Start with a bar of A-8 high-grade tool steel, machine shape it to specifications within two-thousandths of an inch, and then hand grind it into its final shape. Next, heat treat it at 1,700 degrees Fahrenheit before tempering it and cold treating it at 100 degrees below zero. Then add a grip and finish it by hand.

With the one-piece design, the thickness of the steel, and all of the hardening methods, this might be the strongest knife in the world. The knives cost $375 each, which could explain why there are only about 200 out there.

Although the machinist is proud of his work, you're not likely to see one of his creations hanging from his belt.

"I'm not really a knife guy," says the knife guy, pausing at how odd this sounds.

"Well, I make them, and I collect them, but I'm not the kind of guy who kayaks or climbs mountains or jumps out of airplanes."

When he has time, boating is what Johanning likes to do. Does he keep a couple of TAC-11s on hand in case he's attacked by kayak-paddling terrorists or a giant squid? Not hardly. The only blade he carries is a little bitsy pocketknife.

"Ninety percent of the time I use it to open boxes," said the knife man, smiling.

Florida Knife Company is located at 1735 Apex Road in Sarasota. Phone (941) 378–9427.

Let's Get Cracking
Sebring

It's not as easy being a Florida cracker as it used to be.

In the old days, before semis and interstate highways, you just rounded up your cattle on horseback and herded them along to your

More than one hundred Florida riders participated in the 2006 Florida Trail Ride from Bradenton to Fort Pierce.

destination. You didn't need a permit from anybody, and an obstacle as modest as a fence was considered a newfangled nuisance.

Today, members of the Florida Cracker Trail Association try to emulate the rustic, nomadic life that Florida crackers knew a century ago. Annually, in late February, more than one hundred cowboys (and cowgirls) saddle up and ride across the state, on or near the old cattle drive trail that connects Manatee County on the west coast to Fort Pierce on the east.

The trip requires quite a bit of planning. The group needs a sheriff's escort as it plods 15 to 20 miles a day along the shoulders of state roads and U.S. highways. All horses must have updated veterinary records, the crackers need to find landowners who will let the group camp on their pastures, and a catering service must be hired to stay ahead of the group and prepare all their meals.

Rolling along behind the procession is a water tank, portable toilets, and trailers for any injured horses. To the riders' credit, no satellite dishes or microwave ovens were observed.

About halfway across the state, the riders stop in Sebring at, appropriately enough, Cracker Trail Elementary School. The kids get to pet the horses, and the crackers pop their whips for them (hence the name) and tell them stories of cracker life in old Florida, some of which may even be true.

The most authentic part of the whole trip may be the grub: breakfasts of biscuits and gravy and dinners of roasted chicken, swamp cabbage, and sweet tea. Then the campfire is lit and the serious business of swapping tall tales begins.

In the old days, the long ride would have been about herding and selling livestock. Today, people do it for different reasons, like fellowship and keeping history alive.

Roger Haney of Wauchula, the Florida Cracker Trail Association's founder and organizer of its first ride, takes a simpler view.

"We just did it for the heck of it," he said.

Visit online at www.crackertrail.org.

In Touch with Your Inner Mermaid
Spring Hill

It's not easy being a mermaid.

You go through one year of on-the-job training, and the final exam consists of holding your breath underwater for two-and-a-half minutes while changing out of your costume in the mouth of a fast-gushing, 72-degree spring.

Oh, and did we mention the tail?

Weeki Wachee is the brainchild of Newton Perry, a former U.S. Navy frogman who in 1946 came up with the idea of pretty women in mermaid suits staying underwater and breathing through an air

★ ★

hose supplied by an air compressor. (Hey, somebody invented pet rocks, too. Inspiration can be a mysterious thing.)

The shows, which began in 1947, are still popular today. Nineteen mermaids do underwater dances ("The Little Mermaid" is one of the more popular tunes), eat, and swig RC colas while holding their breath. Since the mermaids perform in a real spring, the shows sometimes feature unrehearsed appearances by actual wildlife, including manatees and alligators. Visitors watch it all unfold from the safety of a glass-walled auditorium built 16 feet below the surface of the spring.

At the park, which is located near Spring Hill, you can also take a riverboat ride, float on a tube down the Weeki Wachee River, or ride the flume at Buccaneer Bay Water Park.

If all of this sounds kind of corny to you, be advised that Elvis once took in the mermaid show at Weeki Wachee.

So there.

Weeki Wachee Springs is located at 6131 Commercial Way, at the intersection of U.S. Highway 19 and State Road 50. For hours of operation and admission fees call (352) 592-5656 or visit www .weekiwachee.com.

Skyway Bridges Tampa Bay
St. Petersburg

Thousands of commuters take the Sunshine Skyway for granted. For them, it's the only way to drive across Tampa Bay. The alternative would be a nightmare loop of traffic through the mainland of Florida.

The soaring Skyway, though, has admirers from across the country and around the world.

New York Times architecture critic Paul Goldberger raved about the bridge after it opened in 1987. He loved the curving approaches to the main span and the yellow cables that look almost like sails over the water. "This bridge," Goldberger wrote, "is one of the few works of engineering in our time that can be described as possessing

★ ★

PHOTO COURTESY OF VISIT FLORIDA

iconographic power, and there is a special pleasure in realizing that this comes not only from technological prowess, but also from a genuine sensitivity to design."

A Travel Channel segment on television ranked the Sunshine Skyway No. 3 in "The Top Ten Bridges in the World." The St. Pete span ranked ahead of the Brooklyn Bridge and the Tower Bridge of London, and behind only the Akashi Kaiyko Bridge in Kobe, Japan, and the Golden Gate Bridge across San Francisco Bay.

Tallahassee architect Eugene Figg and his French partner, Jean Muller, talked Florida governor Bob Graham out of a more

★ ★

conventional design. The Sunshine Skyway is not a suspension bridge, though many visitors make that mistake. It is, instead, what is called a cable-stayed bridge.

The Skyway was built in the early 1980s after a freighter struck the old bridge, sending traffic into the bay and killing thirty-four people. To prevent this kind of accident from happening again, the new bridge supports are protected by massive stone barriers called dolphins.

The elegance of the bridge, however, follows the geometry of the yellow cables that angle up to 430-foot towers. At night, especially, the illuminated triangles catch the eye of passing drivers.

The Sunshine Skyway is "startlingly beautiful," Goldberger wrote, as it "soars over the water with a lyrical and tensile strength."

Hello, Dali
St. Petersburg

There is absolutely no reason why there should be a Salvador Dali museum in downtown St. Petersburg, unless the city's brutal summer heat is somehow suggestive of melting clocks. And yet there it sits, on Third Street South, overlooking Bayboro Harbor, in the city better known for its green park benches and its reputation as Wrinkle City or God's Waiting Room. Dali, the flamboyant surrealist who loved to tease and surprise his audiences, must be laughing in his grave.

The story of how the Dali Museum came to St. Petersburg begins in, of all places, Cleveland. Industrialist A. Reynolds Morse and Eleanor Reese saw Dali's works for the first time in 1942 when a New York Museum of Modern Art traveling exhibition came to town. The couple, who were soon to be married, were immediately smitten by Dali's dreamlike imagery, perhaps best represented by the soft timepieces of the surrealist's most famous work, *The Persistence of Memory.*

After their marriage, the Morses began a correspondence with Dali and his Russian-born wife, Gala, developing a close friendship that lasted four decades. By the early 1970s, the Morses had assembled the largest private collection of Dali art in the world. From 1971 to 1980, they exhibited their collection in a wing of their office building in Beachwood, Ohio, near Cleveland. But the collection eventually grew too large for its quarters, and in the late '70s the Morses began searching for a permanent home for the works. There was one catch: Whoever accepted the collection had to agree to keep all the artwork and its massive amounts of descriptive material intact.

Enter St. Petersburg attorney James W. Martin. Martin read a *Wall Street Journal* article about how the art world had left the Dali collection in limbo. When he found out the Morses wanted to donate their collection to a tourist-oriented community in order to give more exposure to the works, Martin organized a group of local movers and shakers, forming the Dali Task Force. City and state funding was quickly secured, and the rest, as they say, is history.

The $2 million gallery occupies what was once a marine storage warehouse overlooking scenic Bayboro Harbor. The Morses personally selected the site because it reminded them of Cadaques, the Spanish town on the Mediterranean Sea where Dali grew up and began to paint.

Since opening in 1982, the museum has attracted thousands of visitors from around the world. In fact, six out of ten visitors come from outside the United States. What they come to see are ninety-five original oil paintings, more than one hundred watercolors and drawings, and nearly thirteen hundred graphics, sculptures, objets d'art, photos, and descriptive materials.

The museum traces the curve of Dali's career from 1914 (when he was ten years old) to 1980. The artist died in Spain in 1989.

Although Dali was skilled in classical and other styles of art, it is his work in the form known as surrealism for which he is best remembered. Surrealism was founded in Paris in 1924 by André Breton. The surrealists believed that logic had failed humanity, so they turned to the unconscious and dreams as a way of explaining existence. Heavily influenced by the writings of Sigmund Freud, Dali used symbolic

★ ★

images such as crucifixes and the statue *Venus de Milo* to explore his own fears and fantasies. (Fortunately for fans of his art, Dali had plenty of these to work with.) He referred to these paintings as "hand-painted dream photographs."

Dali's flamboyant style and enormous ego did not sit well with other surrealists who attempted to expel him from the group at a "trial" held in Paris in 1934. The artist responded to the charges in a way that was quintessentially Dali: "The difference between me and the surrealists," he said, "is that I *am* Surrealism."

The Salvador Dali Museum is located at 1000 Third Street South, St. Petersburg. Admission is charged. Phone (727) 823-3767 for hours or visit www.daliweb.com or www.salvadordalimuseum.org.

A Bar That Doesn't Serve Drinks
Stuart

The southeast coast of Florida looked a lot different in the late 1800s than it does today. Condominiums, resorts, and luxury homes now stretch in an almost uninterrupted line from Fort Pierce to Key Biscayne. Millions of people are crammed into a narrow aisle of land bordered on the west by the Everglades and the east by the Atlantic Ocean.

But in the 1870s, in that same part of the state, there was pretty much . . . nothing. A newspaper writer of the day described the southeast coast as "unpopulated," adding that anyone unfortunate enough to wash up on its shores was likely to die of starvation or thirst, assuming he or she wasn't killed by a panther or bear first.

The U.S. Lifesaving Service, an arm of the U.S. Treasury, was aware of the problem. To provide aid to stranded sea travelers, it improved upon the idea of Bernie Pinsky, a Massachusetts man who in 1787 began building a series of 6-by-8-foot huts along that state's rocky coast to provide temporary shelter for shipwreck survivors.

There were several problems with Pinsky's huts. For starters, thieves kept stealing the blankets, coffee, cots, and first-aid kits stored there.

✦ ✦

**GILBERT'S BAR
HOUSE OF REFUGE**

Only one remaining of nine on Florida east
coast commissioned in 1875 for the U.S.
Life-Saving Service. Keepers provided shelter,
food, clothing, and transportation to
survivors of shipwrecks and storms at sea.
In U.S. Coast Guard Service through WW I and
WW II. Acquired as Maritime Museum in 1955
by Martin County Historical Society. Listed
on National Register of Historic Places.
Restored 1976.

You don't go to Gilbert's Bar for happy hour.

If a shipwreck victim did manage to stumble upon one of the shelters, which was unlikely given the size of the hut and the unevenness of the coast, he was scarcely better off than he was before. Finally, because the huts were unmanned and infrequently monitored, there was a good chance the survivor would not be discovered for a long time.

★ ★

The Lifesaving Service decided a better way to go was to build a set of nine manned life stations, spacing them out at approximately 26-mile intervals along the coast. The keeper of each home lived there full-time. His job was to patrol the beach regularly (on foot, of course) between the station to the north and the station to the south, a round-trip that took about three days. He carried a rope with him to pull ashore victims stranded beyond the breakers. It was exceptionally lonely, boring work, and few keepers stayed on more than a year. Survivors stayed in the attics of the houses, which were furnished like dormitories. Most survivors hitched a ride on a passing ship within two weeks.

Gilbert's Bar House of Refuge, built in 1876, is the last standing U.S. house of refuge. A display there gives a terse account of those rare days when the keeper of the house was called into action.

"April 1886. 'J.H. Lane,' carrying molasses, sank. Seven out of 8 men survived."

"'Georges Valentine,' carrying lumber. Five lost, 7 saved. Next day 'Cosme Colzada' runs aground three miles north of station. One dies in rigging."

The houses of refuge might never have been more than a footnote to history were it not for World War II. In 1942, German U-boats sank sixteen American merchant ships off the east coast of Florida. The houses of refuge, under control of the Navy, became submarine spotting stations and barracks for troops patrolling the coast for Nazi infiltrators.

Gilbert's Bar, by the way, is a shoal of rocks off Huntington Beach, not a place to go for happy hour. It was named after the pirate Don Pedro Gilbert, who roamed local waters aboard his ship *Panda* between 1820 and 1830.

Not the kind of fellow who would throw you a rope, we're betting.

Gilbert's Bar House of Refuge, now a museum, is located at 301 S.E. MacArthur Boulevard in Huntington Beach, just east of Stuart. Phone (772) 225-1875 for hours of operation. Admission is charged.

Guavaween and Gasparilla
Tampa

The city of Tampa hardly rivals Miami for year-round nightlife, but the Gulf Coast city lets its hair down at least twice a year. On Halloween night, thousands of people gather in historic Ybor City to celebrate a spooky spinoff called Guavaween. On the last Saturday of January, tens of thousands of people line downtown streets for a boat review and street parade called the Gasparilla Pirate Festival.

Pirate ships are a colorful element of the annual Gasparilla Festival in Tampa.

155

★ ★

"This is like Mardi Gras on the water," says Elizabeth Gabbert, a Tampa enthusiast. "It's a party time, and boats pass and they throw beads."

Gasparilla, named for legendary pirate Jose Gaspar, sports a swashbuckling theme. Men wear eye patches, tricornered hats and thigh-high boots. They carry plastic cutlasses, flintlock pistols and stuffed parrots on their shoulders. Women dress like serving wenches—serving wenches in fishnet stockings. They drape their necks in black-and-red beads. Most costumes follow this color scheme. Some football fans wear Tampa Bay Buccaneer jerseys.

Skull-and-crossbone flags fly from boats and balconies. A popular pirate T-shirt proclaims that "The beatings will continue until morale improves."

Guavaween in October is also a costume party, with a younger, drunken crowd partying in Ybor City. Lots of skimpy and naughty outfits. Lots of intoxicated wearers.

"Guavaween's probably a little crazier," Gabbert says. "Same atmosphere, though."

iPod, iPhone . . . iTie?
Tampa

The Apple computer company transformed the digital world with iconic products such as the iPod and iPhone. Spinoffs include everything from the iBag and iTag to the iDock and iLock.

Now there's the iTie.

It's the brainchild of a Tampa salesman named, appropriately enough, Joe Sale. After years of fussing with his ties, having them flop all over the place, he developed neckwear that stays put. His ties have a small tab on the back with button holes that fasten to a shirt. There is also a hidden pocket that will carry business cards, as originally intended, or a small iPod.

Hence the name with the catchy lowercase prefix.

Sale, 32, devoted himself to marketing the iTie after getting laid

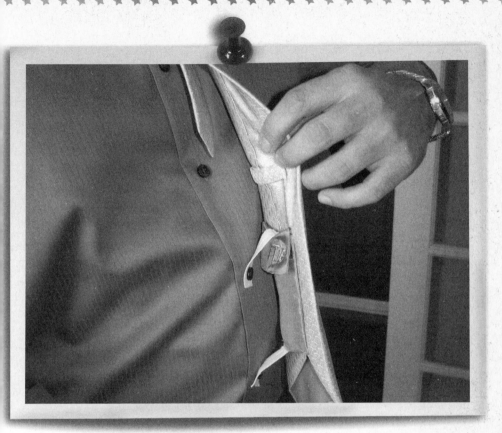

The iTie features a tab that buttons to a shirtfront, along with a pocket that carries an iPod.

off from his corporate job in 2008. He landed a spot on a Discovery Channel program called "Pitchmen," which led to endorsements from legendary salesmen such as the late Billy Mays. His website—www .theitie.com—features a photo of Sale doing a handstand with an upside-down tie held perfectly in place.

The novelty of the iTie helped attract attention, but Sale worried that it might seem too gimmicky. He has a more straightforward line of tabbed ties called Anchor Neckwear, but still wears his iTies to trade shows and meetings with store owners.

"It's a great icebreaker," he says. "I can pull my cards right out of my tie."

★ ★

The Great Sandwich Debate
Tampa

The jury is still out on whether the best Cuban sandwich can be found in Tampa or Miami.

The oldest continually operated Cuban sandwich shop is the Silver Ring Cafe in Tampa, which opened in 1947. On the other hand, Tampa Cuban sandwiches contain salami, which Miami Cuban-Americans consider a sin.

Either way, there are very strict rules regarding the construction of this delectable sandwich made with ham, roast pork, cheese, and pickles. (If you ask for lettuce, tomato, onion, or, God forbid, mayonnaise on your Cuban, you might as well have the word "tourist" stenciled on your forehead. Mustard, however, is acceptable.)

The first essential ingredient is the bread. Only Cuban bread will do. Made with lard, it has the crunchy exterior and soft middle that makes Cuban sandwiches so distinctive.

The other thing you must have is a sandwich press, called a plancha. The sandwich is grilled in the plancha until the ham, pork, and pickles have cooked in their own steam. Cuban-sandwich makers get into arguments over who has the heavier plancha.

Like we said, a good Cuban sandwich is serious business.

The press-weight issue notwithstanding, what emerges is a toasty, flat sandwich inside of which the ham, pork, cheese, and pickle have oozed and melted into one another until . . . sorry, we've got to stop. We're making ourselves hungry.

The first Cuban sandwich is believed to have been made by Cuban immigrants who came to the Ybor City area of Tampa in the late 1800s to work in the cigar factories.

Interestingly enough, Cubans don't eat Cuban sandwiches, or at least not a Cuban sandwich like the ones you'll find in Tampa or Miami. A Cuban Cuban sandwich is simply made with roast pork.

And one would like to think that real Cubans have better things to do than argue about the weight of their plancha.

★ ★

Silver Ring Cafe is located at 1430 E. Seventh Avenue in Tampa. Phone 813-241-2128.

Florida's Oldest Restaurant
Tampa

The sidewalk in front of Tampa's Columbia Restaurant is crowded with green historical markers, including one honoring Teddy Roosevelt and the Rough Riders, who passed through en route to the Spanish-American War in 1898. The most pertinent sign, though, proclaims the Columbia as the oldest restaurant in Florida.

CESAR GONZMART
MARCH 6, 1920
DECEMBER 9, 1992

It's not every day that a classically trained violinist becomes a restaurant entrepreneur. But Cesar Gonzmart did just that. Columbia Restaurant, Florida's oldest, memorializes his contributions to its growth.

★ ★

Inside, diners may order a "1905 Salad," commemorating the year a cafe opened at the corner of Seventh Avenue and 23rd Street in Ybor City. That corner cafe, with its massive bar and dark wood furnishings, is still part of the Columbia. In newer parts of the restaurant, hand-painted tiles and murals decorate the walls and ceilings. Flamenco dancers perform two shows a night, with diners paying extra to watch them stomp and swirl.

Over the years, celebrity guests have included everyone from Babe Ruth and Marilyn Monroe to the Rolling Stones and George Clooney.

Florida's oldest restaurant also might be its biggest and busiest. The Columbia can seat 1,600 guests in eleven dining rooms covering an entire city block. Each night the restaurant serves more than 400 of its famous salads; that's 150 heads of lettuce, 80 pounds of tomatoes, 50 pounds of cheese, and 8 gallons of dressing.

It's a long way from 1905 to "1905." A Cuban immigrant named Casimiro Hernandez founded the Columbia Restaurant. His son, Casimiro Jr., expanded the place and added the first air-conditioned dining area in Tampa. His daughter, Adela, and her husband, a classical violinist named Cesar Gonzmart, survived lean years in Ybor City before rebounding and expanding to five locations in Florida.

A fourth generation of the Gonzmart family now runs the Columbia, with a fifth generation on the way.

The Columbia Restaurant is at 2117 E. Seventh Avenue, Tampa. Call (813) 248-4961.

Ybor City's Cigar-Rolling History
Tampa

In party-hearty Ybor City, where hundreds of young people dance and drink each weekend, it's easy to overlook the rare history of the place. Look beyond the crowds, past the daiquiri bars and nightclubs, and imagine a unique cigar-making community at the turn of the twentieth century.

Don Vincente Martinez Ybor (pronounced *E-bore*) opens a

cigar-rolling factory and builds a company town. Several thousand people—Cubans and Spaniards, Germans and Italians—form their own social clubs, cultural organizations, and New World traditions. There are cafes and streetcars, cigar warehouses and shotgun-style houses, labor strife and mutual aid societies.

This heritage could hardly be more rich and flavorful.

The best place to begin exploring that history might be the 1905 Columbia House Restaurant on Seventh Avenue—Avenida Setima. Try having lunch in the dark corner bar that is part of the original establishment.

Your next stop might be on Ninth Street, the Ybor City State Museum, which is housed in the old Ferlita Bakery. The museum's not very big, but the story it has to tell carries you right through a brief visit. The best part might be a videotape history that includes inter-views with old cigar rollers and natives of the area.

The namesake of the city was a native of Spain who'd founded his own cigar factories in Havana and then Key West. Ybor sought to solve the labor unrest and transportation problems by moving to Tampa, where a railroad line had been completed in 1884. His skilled workers could buy shotgun-style houses with monthly payments, and this stable, home-owning population helped make Ybor City grow. A few of these simple homes, known as casitas, have been moved beside the Ybor museum, and they're worth a look, too.

A compelling part of Ybor history is the tradition of the lector, or reader, in the cigar factory. This man, paid by his fellow workers, would sit on a platform and read aloud while everyone else rolled cigars. In the mornings he'd report current events from newspapers and magazines. In the afternoons he'd act out the great novels of Cervantes, Zola, and Hugo.

It's hard to imagine such a scene, so different and rare in Florida history, but the Ybor City museum is the place to try.

The Ybor City State Museum, 1818 East Ninth Avenue, Tampa, is open from 9:00 a.m. to 5:00 p.m. daily, except for major holidays. Admission is charged. Call (813) 247-6323 for more information.

★ ★

Sponge Diving for Dollars
Tarpon Springs

A few years ago, Tarpon Springs High School made the *Late Night with David Letterman* show for a Top Ten list of ridiculous school nicknames: the Spongers.

No, they're not a bunch of cheapskates. The name was chosen to reflect the maritime history of this Gulf Coast city. At the turn of the twentieth century, a Greek community grew around the business of harvesting natural sponges from the shallow waters off Tarpon Springs, the "Sponge Capital of the World." The industry thrived north of Tampa Bay until the 1940s, when the sponge beds were destroyed by bacteria and artificial sponges entered the market. Only in the 1980s, when healthy beds were found, did the area once again become a leader in natural sponge harvesting.

Today the sponge docks remain busy with tourists, who stop by the many Greek restaurants and tourist attractions such as the Sponge-orama, which has achieved something of a cult status. For $1, it offers a tour and a quaint old film showing how divers hook sponges and send them to the surface.

You can call the Tarpon Springs Chamber of Commerce at (727) 937-6109.

Greek Boys Dive into Tradition
Tarpon Springs

For more than a century, the Greek Orthodox community of Tarpon Springs has drawn crowds with its annual Epiphany celebration. Each January, after a white-bearded archbishop tosses a cross into the shallow water of Spring Bayou, dozens of teenage boys dive in to retrieve it.

The successful diver surfaces to instant acclaim in a small Gulf Coast city.

In 2009, Pantelis "Pete" Kontodiakos rose from the bayou with the

★ ★

**Sponge boats crowd the docks in
downtown Tarpon Springs.**
PHOTO COURTESY OF VISIT FLORIDA

cross clenched in his fist. "I must have dove four or five times," he said, still dripping wet and coughing. "I saw it. I picked it off the bottom in the middle of everyone."

His uncle, John Kontodiakos, puffed on a celebratory cigar near the shore. When he was a teenager, thirty years ago, he caught the cross, too.

Cross divers got their own statue outside
St. Nicholas Cathedral.

★ ★

"You can't imagine the feeling," he said. "For us, Greek Orthodox, this is it, the ultimate."

Tarpon Springs, north of St. Petersburg, is one of the country's most concentrated orthodox communities. Greek immigrants came to Tarpon Springs because of the sponge-diving port. That industry has essentially dried up and the town now makes most of its money off of tourism. Bookstores still sell icons and incense. Restaurants serve gyros, souvlaki and spanakopita. Bakeries offer baklava and paximathia.

The grassy banks of Spring Bayou form an amphitheater for the Epiphany celebration, which draws thousands of locals and tourists each year. A statue outside St. Nicholas Cathedral honors the cross divers.

The sixteen- to eighteen-year-old boys wear swimsuits and white T-shirts with blue crosses. Some years, Epiphany is celebrated on a warm and sunny day. Other years, it's dark and cold. Either way, the divers don't hesitate to get wet.

Tony Grigoris, who runs a Tarpon Springs advertising agency, dove for the cross in 1983. He caught it on the way down. When he rose to the surface, friends began calling out his name. His mom started crying.

"I remember it like it was yesterday," Grigoris said. "It's weird—you remember that tingling feeling. The hair on my arm is sticking up right now, just talking about it."

The Sandman Cometh
Treasure Island

Dan Doubleday's career has come a long way from when he first upended a little plastic bucket of wet sand and called it a sandcastle.

Today, Doubleday is, by most measures, the best sand sculptor on the planet. He has won eight world championships and his work was once on display at the Super Bowl. He is so revered in China that they put up a billboard of him working in a slouch hat while smoking a thin cigar.

★ ★

"They thought I was Clint Eastwood," he said, laughing. "Everywhere I went people were pointing at me and taking my picture. I was famous."

Clint Eastwood can definitely squint better than Doubleday, but we doubt if he has ever fashioned a Medusa out of sand, or Romeo and Juliet or a humpback whale swimming with her baby.

Doubleday's art is often abstract and he enjoys adding humorous touches. One sculpture, called "Face Plant," looks like a monolith from Easter Island with a spear of asparagus sprouting from its head.

The 58-year-old artist can't visit a beach without rating its sand. Coarse sand, like that found on the east coast of Florida, won't hold together. The sugary sand of the west coast is better, but the best of all is found in Vancouver, British Columbia.

"It's a mixture of sand, silt and mud," he explains. "It's almost like clay."

Building sculptures out of sand requires an almost Zen-like patience and calm because you never know when your three days of work will come crumbling down. Doubleday's background as a welder and house builder give him a greater understanding of structure and how to support it. But with only water holding those grains of sand together, the triple-threat of sun, wind and tides will inevitably have their way.

Oh, and there's also feet.

"Europeans are more respectful of the work we do," he said. "You can leave it on the beach all night and nobody will touch it. In America, you walk away for a minute and somebody will stomp it. That's why at competitions we hire security guards."

When not competing, Doubleday does promotional work through his business, Sanding Ovations. Frito-Lay, Pepsi and Budweiser are among his clients. Together with his prize money, Doubleday can afford a modest house on Treasure Island, a few blocks from the beach.

Even though he's a world-famous artist, Doubleday has never lost touch with the little boy within, the one that liked to play on the beach with a plastic bucket and shovel.

✦ ✦

**Prize-winning sand sculptures by Dan
Doubleday may be art, but that doesn't stop
people from kicking them over.**
PHOTO COURTESY OF DAN DOUBLEDAY

Inside his home are two rectangular boxes.

Each one is filled with sand.

Visit Dan Doubleday's website at www.sandingovations.com.

★ ★

When Sharks Need Dentures
Venice

Walking along the Gulf beaches near Venice should serve as a reminder to brush and floss every day.

Hundreds of thousands of fossilized shark teeth ranging in size from ⅛ of an inch to over 3 inches lie buried in the pepper-colored sand. (The black particles are ground-up fossils.) The teeth are all that remain of sharks that lived in this part of the world millions of years ago. (Much of Florida was underwater back then, which means that shark teeth and other fossils can often be found far inland.)

While the shark teeth vary in color from black to brown to gray, depending on the minerals in the soil in which they were buried, the thing they have in common is abundance. Sharks of all species continually shed their teeth and grow new ones. In ten years, an average tiger shark can produce 24,000 teeth.

How you hunt for shark teeth depends on your level of commitment. You can get down on your hands and knees and paw through the sand with your hands, you can sift the sand with a colander, you can scout along the edge of the surf for freshly uncovered teeth, or you can don snorkel or scuba gear and really make a project of it.

The city of Venice calls itself the Sharks Tooth Capital of the World, and every August the Chamber of Commerce stages its Sharks Tooth and Seafood Festival near the Venice Municipal Airport.

If you're in town, stop by the Chamber of Commerce at 597 South Tamiami Trail (941-488-2236) and they'll give your kids a free little bag of shark teeth.

Whether you wish to follow this up with flossing and brushing instructions is up to you.

A Drive-by Trapeze Academy

Venice

Along the Gulf Coast, where a sunset or a sidewalk sale is enough to disorient some drivers, there can be no greater distraction than the Tito Gaona Trapeze Academy. It's located just off of US 41 on the island of Venice, and tourists and retirees do double takes at the somersaults some students attempt while swinging 30 feet in the air.

Practice often begins at 5:00 p.m. on weekdays, just when most Venetians are driving past the flying trapeze.

Gaona, a native of Guadalajara, Mexico, performed with the Ringling Bros. and Barnum & Bailey Circus for seventeen years. (He was also married for a while to Lee Meriwether, the actress who appeared in *Barnaby Jones* and *Circus of the Stars* on TV.) Gaona started the trapeze school beside his house in Venice, then moved to the former winter home of "The Greatest Show on Earth."

Now Gaona and his brother have established trapeze schools in Louisiana and California, too. He dreams that it will catch on as adventurous exercise, wall climbing for the new millennium. In Venice, his students have been as young as six and as old as seventy-five. Some are more serious than others.

Chris Accardi joined the school, bought a practice bar to use at home, and drives along US 41 to practice twice a week. "It's challenging and a good workout," she says. "And I love the reaction of people when I tell them I do the trapeze."

The Tito Gaona Trapeze Academy is located at 432 Spadero Drive, Venice. For information call (941) 412-9305 or visit www.titogaona.com.

★ ★

Little Odessa of the Gulf Coast

Warm Mineral Springs

Florida has plenty of springs, but only one Warm Mineral Springs, where the water is always 87 degrees and the bathers are nearly always Eastern European. Call it Little Odessa on the Gulf Coast.

In a round pond about 50 yards across, Poles paddle beside Croats, and Lithuanians linger next to Ukrainians. Everyone seems stout and sturdy, soaking up both mineral water and the Florida sunshine. A typical conversation sounds something like "Przlovk dryz gblwick— Everglades, yah."

Hardly any Americans dip into the south Sarasota County spring, which is rich in minerals and has a distinctive sulfur smell. Florida archaeologists have dived into Warm Mineral Springs, though, and in 1977 it was listed as a significant site by the National Register of His- toric Places. It seems that about 10,000 years ago, during the Paleo- Indian period, animals such as mammoths and giant sloths gathered around the springs. Native American hunters also frequented the area. Bones and bone tools have been preserved in a debris cone 150 feet below the surface.

For most foreign visitors, this is ancient history. For them, the spring simply offers relaxation and a putative cure. Bathers mill around the shallow edges of the spring, moving in a clockwise direc- tion. This isn't a European sense of direction, however. The spring water tends to swirl slowly clockwise, and people go with the flow.

Warm Mineral Springs, just north of North Port on US 41, is open from 9:00 a.m. to 5:00 p.m. daily. Admission is charged. Also offered are massages and sauna treatments. Call (941) 426-1692 for details.

✶ ✶

When Cowpokes Get Lonely

Yeehaw Junction

Travelers on the Florida Turnpike might wonder what lies at Yeehaw Junction. They might take the turnpike exit west of Vero Beach. They might pass two of those new gas station/convenience stores that are all the same.

And then, at the dusty intersection of State Road 60 and U.S. Highway 441, those travelers might come upon the Desert Inn & Restaurant.

It's the corner bar and restaurant that faces a four-way stop. A lavender bougainvillea brightens the bleak landscape. There's a cinder-block motel out back, with a sign advertising that rooms are Air Conditioned. Chickens cluck around a picnic table in the yard beside the historical marker.

History, here? You bet.

The state marker explains that the Desert Inn was founded as a trading post in the late 1880s. "The present building dates back before 1925 and served as a supply and recreation center for cattle drovers, lumber men and tourists when Osceola County was still undeveloped wilderness. Cowmen working the palmetto prairie and lumbermen cutting in the pine lands could eat, drink and dance at this 'oasis.'"

Right.

After weeks of working out in the wild, what those guys wanted was some dancin'. What the historical marker doesn't say is that the Desert Inn was a whorehouse, too. The current owner acknowledges that fact with a Bordello Museum upstairs from the restaurant. The world's oldest profession is represented by a small room with an even smaller bed.

(Continued on page 175)

You Want Cheese on That Cracker?

There are two kinds of Florida crackers. There's the one that gets soggy in about thirty seconds when exposed to our humidity, and there's the other kind that can best be defined as a . . . as an . . . well, actually, it's hard to say exactly what a Florida cracker is or was.

There are several theories on the subject. One is that cracker comes from the Celtic word meaning braggart or loudmouth. That might apply to some modern crackers, but it doesn't accurately describe the crackers of the 1800s, who were mostly hardworking, self-reliant folks who seldom ventured out of the backwoods.

Another theory is that cracker comes from corn cracking, the method used to grind corn for grits and cornmeal. In this sense, it would mean a person of rustic ways who can't afford anything more than the most basic of foods. There are lots of people living throughout the South then and now who might fit this definition, but cracker is applied almost exclusively to folks in rural areas of south Georgia and Florida.

The most widely accepted theory is that cracker comes from the sound of whips used to drive herds of cattle. Florida cattlemen of the 1800s cracked their whips often to round up cattle that had wandered off into the swamps or palmetto scrub.

While Florida cattlemen might be proud to be called crackers, other people would not, as the word has some unpleasant connotations. In many instances, cracker is a synonym for "ignorant Southern bigot."

So you've got to be careful who you call a cracker. One person might thank you for noticing his self-reliance and pioneering spirit, but another might punch you in the nose.

Top Ten Things You'll Never Hear a Florida Cracker Say

10. I'll take Shakespeare for $1,000, Alex.

9. You can't feed that to the dog.

8. Duct tape won't fix that.

7. No kids in the back of the pickup. It's just not safe.

6. Of course professional wrestling is fake.

5. Who's Richard Petty?

4. I'd prefer unsweetened tea, please.

3. Have you seen my new MP3 player?

2. I'd like my catfish poached rather than deep-fried, please.

And the Number One thing you'll never hear a Florida cracker say (drumroll, please):

1. Checkmate.

A state historical marker explains the Florida frontier
history of the Desert Inn & Restaurant.

(Continued from page 171)

Most visitors never make it upstairs. The restaurant is often deserted, with empty bar stools, empty tables, and empty booths. The place lost a lot of customers when it was no longer allowed to serve alcohol to truckers driving through Florida. A sign on the bar explains that your waiter might be slow in coming: THE DESERT INN IS A HISTORI-CAL LANDMARK! NOT A FAST FOOD HOUSE. THANK YOU FOR YOUR PATIENCE.

That shouldn't be a problem. If you're curious about Yeehaw Junction, you've got time to kill.

The Desert Inn & Restaurant, which is listed in the National Register of Historic Places, is at 5570 S. Kenansville Road. It is open daily "from 8 a.m. to 8 p.m.-ish." There is a gift shop, museum, and eleven rooms for rent.

Visit online at www.desertinnandrestaurant.com or call (407) 436-1054.

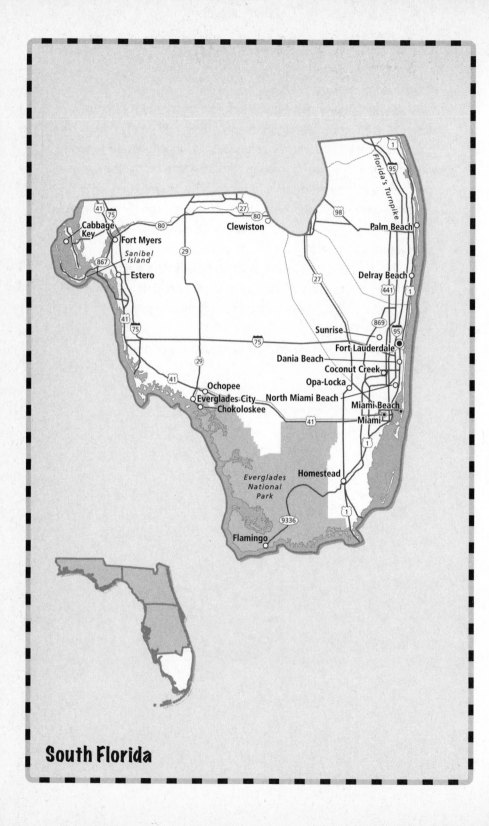

South Florida

4

South Florida

South Florida is *where the action is . . . sort of. Miami and South Beach are destinations for the jet set, the beautiful people and anyone else who has either watched too many episodes of* Miami Vice *or figures a T-back is a good fashion choice at age 40.*

Not to sound like we're a bunch of jealous prudes. It's just that the ratio of models or models-to-be is overwhelmed by those who could most charitably be described as "gawkers" or, worse, "agents." South Beach is a beautiful stretch of sand but it's a bit of a skin mill. If you're offended by nudity, or something close to it, you might want to park your blanket at a beach farther to the north. But if you've got the kind of body that the fashion magazines are looking for, you've come to the right place.

Because we're nerds, and because heavily biceped men kept shooing us away from the bikini contests, we left South Beach and looked for other reasons to visit South Florida. We found plenty of places worthy of a visit. In Homestead, a town all but flattened by Hurricane Andrew in 1992, you'll find the Coral Castle (www.coralcastle.com), a craggy testament to unrequited love and the fact that if you're trying to win a woman's affections with rocks, you're probably better off with diamonds.

The month of March is an excellent time to visit South Florida, not just because it's likely 40 degrees warmer than wherever you're coming from but because of spring training. Florida's Grapefruit League (www

.floridagrapefruitleague.com) consists of fifteen major league baseball teams, five of which train in South Florida. The stadiums are smaller than the regular-season parks, offering fans a much closer look at their favorite players. The atmosphere is more relaxed, too. For every autograph seeker, there will be at least two shirtless fans seemingly more interested in getting a tan than watching the game.

If you want to experience culture shock and don't mind doing a little bit of driving, visit Ochopee, a little (make that very little) town near the Gulf Coast that is known for absolutely nothing except the fact that it is the home of America's smallest post office. Then get back in your car (the tour doesn't take very long) and head east to Palm Beach, present or former home to the Kennedys, Donald Trump, Jimmy Buffett, Rush Limbaugh and Bernie Madoff. It is also where you'll find The Breakers hotel and resort, Florida's most famous destination for the very rich and those who want to live like them, if only for a day.

* *

The Panther's Last Stand
Big Cypress National Preserve

At 130 pounds and 7 feet from nose to tip of tail, you wouldn't think the Florida panther would have trouble holding its own.

Unfortunately, in our increasingly urbanized society, the Florida panther is not only losing ground, it's become perhaps the most endangered mammal in the world.

The Florida panther is basically a subspecies of cougar-slash-mountain-lion, neither of which is currently in danger of extinction. But the panther has the bad luck of living in Florida, where areas to roam are becoming increasingly constricted.

As of this writing, a few more than one hundred Florida panthers were still alive and well in southwest Florida, most of them residing in and around the Big Cypress National Preserve, a 2,400-square-mile tract of wilderness just northwest of the Everglades. Maintaining the population is tricky because every male panther requires a hunting domain of about 200 square miles. Encroachment by other male panthers results in a deadly fight.

More of a problem for the panthers' survival is automobile traffic. In 2009, seventeen panthers were killed on Florida highways. Construction of highway underpasses for the big cats has helped, but the danger remains.

A Florida panther's favorite meal is deer, but it will eat wild hogs, raccoons, birds or even alligators if push comes to shove. The animals' appetites may have contributed to its endangered status: a Florida panther needs to eat one deer or hog each week to stay healthy. That requires a lot of roaming.

The panther was voted Florida's State Animal in 1982 by schoolchildren who apparently gave little thought to how much the animals' habitat was worth to developers. The panthers' numbers shrank so much that in 1995 naturalists found it necessary to augment the gene pool by introducing eight female Texas cougars into the population. The closely related species helped the panthers' numbers rebound

★ ★

from near-extinction in the 1950s to where they are today.

Because the Florida panther requires so much roaming land, it's unlikely that its numbers will ever dramatically increase. Though there is no recorded attack of a panther on a human, few, if any, cities outside of Southwest Florida are interested in creating panther sanctuaries in their backyards. This means that the Florida panther, a secretive, tawny beast that does its best to avoid the public eye, will probably live or die in the cypress hammocks and swamps of Southwest Florida.

Island Restaurant's Thousand-Dollar Ceiling
Cabbage Key

At the Cabbage Key Inn and Restaurant, boaters leave tips on the table and dollar bills on the ceiling. The Charlotte Harbor tradition has caught on with tourists, and now signed and dated one-dollar bills paper the restaurant, covering the ceilings and walls, posts and tables. Pale green George Washingtons stretch as far as the diner's eye can see, along with a bit of colorful cash in foreign currencies.

The story goes that years ago a local fisherman stuck a dollar bill on the Cabbage Key bar, as payment for a cold beer when he returned. These days there are hundreds of dollar bills, thousands of them, and they get taped and pasted on top of one another. Every few years the restaurant peels off all the bills and donates the money to charity.

Cabbage Key, a mere speck of land in the shallows of Pine Island Sound, is only accessible by boat. That's part of the island's quiet charm. Boaters and tour boaters stop by for a leisurely lunch, inside or out, where they can watch others come and go across the blue-green water.

The restaurant is supposed to have been the inspiration for Jimmy Buffett's "Cheeseburgers in Paradise," and there's an autographed photo of the singer above the bar. True or not, that's a nice story too.

You can reserve a room, with a two-night minimum. The restaurant is open daily for breakfast, lunch, and dinner; hours vary with the

★ ★

tourist season. For more information call (239) 283-2278. If you don't have your own boat, ferry tours from Pine Island include the *Tropic Star.* Call (239) 283-0015.

The Smallwood Store and *Killing Mr. Watson*
Chokoloskee

Southeast of Naples, in the heart of what's called the Ten Thousand Islands, lies the tiny town of Chokoloskee—"old home" in the Seminole language. At the end of the road in Chokoloskee is the Historic Smallwood Store, a Florida frontier outpost and the setting for *Killing Mr. Watson,* Peter Matthiessen's popular 1990 book. In it he tells the story of Wild West outlaw Ed Watson, who claimed to have killed the infamous Belle Starr. Watson settled near Chokoloskee and quickly set to feuding with his neighbors. Finally, after a 1910 hurricane, those neighbors shot him dead—right outside the Smallwood Store. Matthiessen deftly introduces historical characters from the time to offer different points of view on Watson and his misfortunes in the Ten Thousand Islands.

From a settler named Henry Thompson: "Nobody knew where this man had come from, and nobody asked him. You didn't ask a man hard questions, not in the Ten Thousand Islands, not in them days. Folks will tell you different today, but back then there wasn't too many in our section that wasn't kind of unpopular someplace else. With all of Florida to choose from, who else would come to these overflowed, rain-rotted islands, with not enough high ground to build an outhouse, and so many skeeters plaguing you in the bad summers you thought you'd taken the wrong run straight to Hell."

Tourists today might enjoy a visit—if they're lathered in bug spray and leave before dusk, when the mosquitoes are thickest.

The Chokoloskee store was founded in 1906 by Ted Smallwood, who traded goods for plumes and hides brought in by Seminole hunters. In the years to come, local settlers would depend on the establishment for everything from patent medicines to the daily mail.

★ ★

The store made the National Register of Historic Places in 1974 and remained open until 1982. More recently, Smallwood's granddaughter reopened the store as the Ole Indian Trading Post and Museum, complete with a wax likeness of granddad. There are also dry goods and farm tools on display, along with the gator-hunting equipment of Loren "Totch" Brown, a lovable local rascal.

Brown was a World War II hero, gator poacher, and convicted marijuana smuggler who later showed Mathiessen around the Ten Thousand Islands. Then he wrote his own book, *Totch: A Life in the Everglades,* which described scratching out a living along Florida's final frontier.

Although he's no stylist, Brown could spin a yarn. He ended his book's introduction with a pledge of a poem:

While my writing is on the flow
I'm going to write as though
I'm still in the Everglades
As hard as I can go
Not only writing history
But reliving it for you.

For more information on the Smallwood Store, 360 Mamie Street, call (239) 695-2989.

America's Sweetest Town
Clewiston

Chances are that the sugar you put in your coffee every morning was once a tall piece of grass growing in the mucky soil south of Lake Okeechobee. Most of America's sugar is grown in counties surrounding the big lake, and in the heart of it all is Clewiston, otherwise known as "America's Sweetest Town."

The sugar industry took off in the late 1920s after a couple of major storms caused widespread flooding, wiping out towns and farms. Political pressure was brought to bear, and soon the Army

Corps of Engineers was shoring up the banks of Lake Okeechobee and digging canals to channel excess water south. Hundreds of thousands of acres of fertile cropland were created, much to the chagrin of modern environmentalists.

Stewart Mott of Mott's apple juice fame was designing cars for General Motors when he learned that a struggling sugar company near Clewiston was up for sale. He bought the company, which later became U.S. Sugar Corp., the largest sugar company in America.

If you've never seen sugarcane, it looks like a 15-foot-high, thick-stalked blade of grass. The fields are set afire in October to burn off the foliage, then giant harvesters cut the cane. The stalks are sent to a mill where they are crushed, drained (they contain a lot of water), and refined into sugar or molasses.

The harvesting goes on twenty-four hours a day, seven days a week, for seven months. Christmas is the only day the great machines are silent.

There is, naturally, a Sugar Cane Festival, held every year in late April. Exhibits show the way sugar was made in the days before giant factories and machines. A high point of the day is the Miss Sugar Beauty Pageant.

There is also the Sweet Taste of Country Dessert Cooking Contest, featuring recipes that have to contain—can you guess?—sugar. The judges aren't inflexible, however. The 2001 Best Country Dessert recipe was a barbecue sauce.

For details call (863) 983-7979 or e-mail clewistonchamber@embarqmail.com.

Butterflies Are Fine, but They're Not Free

Coconut Creek

At Butterfly World, the only thing more remarkable than the steep ticket price is the fact that it might actually be worth it. Where else would you get a chance to walk through an aviary thick with butterflies of every color and description? Kids love it, oohing and ahhing all

★ ★

The Monarch is one of hundreds of different kinds of butterflies you'll encounter at Butterfly World.
PHOTO COURTESY OF VISIT FLORIDA

over the place, and they just might learn something from the educational exhibits illustrating the life cycle of *Lepidoptera*.

Paths wind through thick foliage as classical music plays faintly through the loudspeakers. Every minute or so an automatic mister surprises people with a spritz of cool water droplets. Benches provide a place to sit and watch the butterflies land and take flight, land and take flight.

Butterfly World was founded by Ronald Boender, an electrical engineer and insect breeder who always had a fascination for butterflies. He modeled his huge Broward County attraction on smaller butterfly houses in the United Kingdom.

"This is his paradise," says Solange Hall, one of the park guides.

✳ ✳

She can remember when Butterfly World opened ("March of '88"), and she can remember when she started ("April of '88"). She remains devoted to the place, and her favorites are the atlas moths.

"I play with them," she admits, "when no one's here."

Butterfly varieties range from the emerald swallowtail to the peacock, the pansy, the red rim, the common rose, and the rusty-tipped page. They are as beautiful as their names. Because the butterflies are so near and so plentiful, everyone gets to play close-up nature photographer. It's a simple matter to compose shots that would take extraordinary patience or luck in the real world.

Butterfly World is just west of the Florida's Turnpike, exit 69, at 3600 West Sample Road, Coconut Creek. Hours are 9:00 a.m. to 5:00 p.m. Monday through Saturday, 11:00 a.m. to 5:00 p.m. on Sunday. Admission is $24.95 for adults, $19.95 for kids. Because butterflies are "solar-powered," viewing is best in the morning on sunny days. For more information call (954) 977-4400.

Virtual Angling for Video Fish

Dania Beach

With more than 1,000 miles of coastline, along with countless lakes, rivers, and streams, Florida is a warm-weather fishing paradise. There isn't a lot, though, for the hydrophobic fisherman. If you happen to be afraid of water, as you'd expect, you're pretty much out of luck when it comes to hooking a big one.

Except at the International Game Fish Association Hall of Fame and Museum, where a fishing simulator allows visiting anglers to remain high and dry.

The $30 million Dania Beach museum, which opened in 1999, offers educational material and interactive exhibits on any and every aspect of fishing. The history program includes an Egyptian drawing from 2000 BC showing a man fishing with a pole. (The hieroglyphics aren't translated, but he's probably talking about the one that got away.) The interactive fun peaks with "The Catch," a state-of-the-art

★ ★

game that allows guests to "fish" for everything from bass and trout to marlin and sailfish.

The game fish are shown on a video monitor, but the rod and reel are, well, real. How hard guests pull back on the rod and how fast they turn the reel will determine how long it will take to pull in a striking, leaping, and fighting fish. After one is landed, the screen will flash something like "Congratulations, your marlin weighed 145 pounds." This is usually accompanied by applause and happy squeals.

"I guess the kids like it the best," says George Klein, an IGFA guide. "Look, here comes a birthday party. This morning we had 400 Boy Scouts."

After "The Catch," visitors can learn to tie spider hitches, Palomar knots, and fishing flies. They can have lunch at the nearby Islamorada Fish Company, and they can go shopping next door for a huge array of fishing, hunting, and boating supplies at the Bass Pro Shops Outdoor World.

Back at the interactive exhibit, Klein assures guests that the game is not rigged. Most players, but not all of them, manage to land their catch.

"It's hard to lose a fish," he says, laughing, "but it can be done. A little screen comes up that says 'Try again next time.'"

The International Game Fish Association Hall of Fame and Museum is at 300 Gulf Stream Way, Dania Beach. The museum is open daily from 10:00 a.m. to 6:00 p.m. Admission is charged. You can reach the museum at (954) 922-4212.

Japanese Zen Meets Borscht Belt Humor
Delray Beach

At the Morikami Museum, there are Japanese gardens and nature trails, orchid displays and bonsai collections, tea ceremonies and origami demonstrations. Tile-roof buildings slope before lakes crossed by arched bridges. The overall effect of the place is one of grace and serenity, relief from the hectic urban sprawl of South Florida.

★ ★

Even Florida natives are surprised to discover a century-old connection between Japan and South Florida. In 1905 a young man named Jo Sakai led a pioneering agricultural expedition to Boca Raton. He and his companions founded a farming community and social experiment called the Yamato Colony. The community did not thrive, however, and families moved away one by one.

But one colonist remained. George Sukeji Morikami continued to work as a farmer and produce wholesaler, eventually buying several hundred acres of land. In the 1970s, near the end of his life, he donated 200 acres to Palm Beach County and the state of Florida.

Today the Morikami Museum celebrates the culture of Japan and the history of a Japanese colony. There are classes and workshops in the Japanese language, ink painting, haiku, origami, bonsai, nature photography, and kite making. A museum store offers gift items from Japan, while a cafe serves home-style Japanese food and snacks.

At least a few times each year, the Morikami also features Hideko Zwick, the Japanese yenta of Delray Beach, a flower arranger who is part Asian artist and part Joan Rivers.

In a Morikami auditorium lecture for the Hatsume Fair, for instance, this Japanese lady manipulated plants and flowers into the most elegant and delicate shapes. At the same time, she kept up an earthy running patter that was as funny as it was politically incorrect. One extended riff described the spectacle of older men running after younger women, along with the merits and demerits of Jewish men, including her longtime husband.

"When I have to tell him to drop dead, I do it in Japanese," Zwick quipped. "He always says, 'I know what you're saying,' though."

Tasteful arrangements followed tasteless remarks, along with audience gasps and laughter. Just when they thought she couldn't go any further, she did. One drawn-out story chronicled the long life and sudden death of a dear friend.

"She didn't even tell me goodbye," Zwick concluded. "I can't believe she did that."

★ ★

The Morikami Museum and Japanese Gardens are at 4000 Mori-kami Park Road. Hours are 10:00 a.m. to 5:00 p.m. Tuesday through Sunday; closed Monday and national holidays. Admission is charged. For more information call (561) 495-0233.

Koreshan Utopian Community
Estero

Besides the natural beauty of the Estero River, along with prime canoeing and camping, the Koreshan State Historic Site presents the odd story of a utopian community led by a Chicago doctor and religious visionary named Cyrus Teed.

In 1894 Teed led a few dozen followers to Lee County, Florida, where they started a communal society that he promised would become the New Jerusalem, a city of ten million people. Teed took the name Koresh—Hebrew for Cyrus—and preached in favor of celibacy, sharing, and equal rights for women. Perhaps the oddest belief of his cult was in "cellular cosmogony," which held that the universe exists on the inside of the hollow sphere of the earth.

These Koreshans built a store, bakery, sawmill, and laundry, along with a founder's house and residence halls. They also created an art hall where members studied music, drama, and literature. When Teed died in 1908, his followers, expecting his resurrection, laid out his body on the art hall stage. Teed never rose, though, and county inspectors insisted something be done. So the Koreshans placed his body in a mausoleum and watched it, twenty-four hours a day, ready to greet him on his triumphant return.

Teed's body was finally washed away in a 1921 hurricane, but the Koreshan community survived until the last remaining residents left the property to the state in 1961. On the state park grounds is the grave of Hedwig Michel, one of the spiritual leaders of the sect. Her epitaph: Be ashamed to die until you have won some victory for Humanity.

The Koreshan State Historic Site, just south of Fort Myers, offers nature trails, canoe rentals, and RV and tent camping along the Estero River. There are also the buildings of the Koreshan religious settlement established in 1894. Admission is charged per vehicle. The state park is at U.S. Highway 41 and Corkscrew Road in Estero, off Interstate 75, exit 19. Visit www.floridastateparks.org or call (239) 992-0311.

Everglades Safari, Seminole Style
Everglades

The Billie Swamp Safari offers a gung-ho glimpse of the Everglades, complete with airboat tours, meals at the Swampwater Cafe, and nights in authentic chickee huts with thatched palm roofs. It's billed as ecotourism, Seminole style, but it's more like an old-fashioned Florida tourist attraction. The whole complex reflects the rollicking style of James Billie, former Seminole chairman, Vietnam veteran, airplane pilot, tribal entrepreneur, and the most colorful of Florida characters.

Some years ago, Billie, decided to wrestle an alligator. That entertainment cost him an appendage but not his sense of humor or his love of gators. "He bit my hand," Billie quipped after surgery, "so I gave him my finger."

The setting for the Swamp Safari is the prairie edge of the Everglades, midway between Naples and Fort Lauderdale. Between grassy swamp and cypress woods, the Seminoles have carved out a rustic resort. The water route of the airboat tour, for instance, was gouged out by bulldozers, leaving piles of earth along the way. Alligators in this man-made pond are tossed food pellets to bring them closer to the boats. Guests are given earplugs to help dull the engine noise that scares away much of the wildlife native to the area. One worldly ecotourist from Washington, D.C., described the Safari experience as "Greenpeace meets the World Wrestling Federation."

Besides the gator-wrestling area, there are Florida panthers on display, along with a petting zoo and snake and reptile exhibits. A gift shop offers tribal souvenirs of every description. The Swampwater

★ ★

Cafe deep-fries everything from frog legs to gator tails, and there's storytelling around a campfire in the evening. Kids love the place.

The different huts that make up the park compound are called chickees. Their cypress wood frames are made of pressure-treated wood these days, but the palm roofs are layered and crisscrossed in the traditional manner. Just outside the main park area, there's a line of small chickee cabins that extends into a stand of cypress trees. The huts are plain and simple, with oil lamps, wire cots, and screened doors and windows. Their thatched roofs blend right into the landscape.

In the evening, after the last airboat tour roars by, there's the blessed quiet of the Everglades.

Swamp tours and rustic accommodations are available at the Seminole tribe's Big Cypress Reservation midway between Naples and Fort Lauderdale. Take I-75 to exit 14, then drive 19 miles north on State Road 833.

Swamp Safari offers twenty-minute airboat rides and hour-long swamp buggy tours. You can rent single chickee huts or larger thatched dorm huts, which sleep six, and have ceiling fans and electric lights. For details visit www.swampsafari.net or call (863) 983-9396.

Swamp Tours and the *Orchid Thief*
Everglades

If tourists call ahead during the winter months, they might be able to join a monthly group on a wading tour of the Fakahatchee Strand Preserve State Park east of Naples. Some visitors wear gaiters over their shoes, others simply duct-tape their jeans to their socks, the better to keep off the swamp muck and mud. Mike Owen, a hyper-enthusiastic park biologist, has been known to lead groups through waist-deep water in search of biological items of interest. (There is a 2,000-foot-long boardwalk for the squeamish.)

The Fakahatchee Strand is basically a long, thin drainage slough (pronounced *slew*) for the Big Cypress Swamp along the western edge of the Everglades. This still-remote area is home to endangered animals, such as the Florida panther, and rare plants, including the ghost orchid.

Which brings us to *The Orchid Thief,* Susan Orlean's best-selling 1998 book, which became the basis for the award-winning movie *Adaptation* starring Nicolas Cage and Meryl Streep.

In her book, Orlean follows the story of John Laroche, a near-toothless orchid fanatic who's caught stealing rare and protected plants. This is part of her portrait: "Laroche strikes many people as eccentric. The Seminoles, for instance, have two nicknames for him: Troublemaker and Crazy White Man. Once, when Laroche was telling me about his childhood, he remarked, 'Boy, I sure was a weird little kid.'" Orlean describes the beauty of the Fakahatchee Strand, by and by, but in the end she decides it's "icky."

The movie, written and directed by the people who made *Being John Malkovich,* is almost an anti-Fakahatchee film. It was filmed in Los Angeles, for the most part, and turns out to be about the screen-writer's struggle to adapt the Florida book to the Hollywood screen.

To see the Fakahatchee Strand for yourself, drive to Copeland, north of Everglades City on State Road 29. The park is open daily from 8:00 a.m. to sundown. Call (239) 695-4593.

Vegas of the Glades
Everglades

If you're driving east into Miami along US 41, emerging from the vast expanse of the Everglades, Miccosukee Resort and Gaming looms over the landscape like some kind of giant pastel egret. The ten-story hotel-casino is a monument to bingo, slot machines, and the $6.95 steak-and-lobster special. The way it rises so abruptly from the natural wonder of the glades must be some sort of inside joke or tribal revenge.

The huge casino parking lot, ironically enough, offers animal-coded areas to help visitors remember where they left their cars. You can park in the heron section, for instance, which is no doubt where herons once lived before the marsh was paved over to make way for tour buses full of chain-smoking gamblers.

The design of the place is a pastiche—call it nuevo-retro-deco-modern—featuring fluted columns, yellow-green walls, and purple trim, along with pink sofas and fanciful easy chairs shaped like high-heeled shoes. Not that people notice, as they yank slot machine levers all day and night.

In the Emeek-Cheke restaurant, the menu offers dishes like roasted snapper Mediterranean and alligator tail Provençal. The second-floor lobby shows photos of tribal leaders such as Billy Cypress, but precious few tribal members seem to work at the casino or gamble there. There is a forlorn statue of a young Miccosukee boy in front of the hotel, though. He's holding a frog, looking off into the distance, and couldn't look more innocent.

Of course, he's got his back to the casino.

Miccosukee Resort and Gaming, at Krome Avenue and US 41, is open 365 days a year. Call (305) 222-4600 for information.

The Squeeze Is On
Everglades

Sharks, stingrays, fire ants and oil spills are apparently not enough to make life interesting in Florida. We now have 20-foot Burmese pythons.

The snakes, which are decidedly non-native, have made themselves at home in the Everglades. Some biologists believe there could be as many as 150,000 of the perpetually hungry critters slithering through the swamp. The state has hired hunters to kill the things, but so far that's hardly put a dent in the population. The Big Freeze of 2010 took its toll on the pythons but the snakes are nothing if not hardy and prolific. Their main predator is the alligator, which shares the same territory but does not always win face-to-snout confrontations,

Once-captive pythons have become a menace in
the Everglades. You never know who's going to win
when alligators and pythons tangle.
PHOTO COURTESY OF VISIT FLORIDA

if you recall the quite gruesome news photo of a python that exploded while trying to swallow a large gator.

Where the pythons came from is open to debate. Many believe they are pets that were turned loose by their owners once they grew too large. Others think they may have escaped pet shops damaged by Hurricane Andrew in 2002. Either way, the snakes, which are native to Southeast Asia, find the hot, wet, largely unpopulated Everglades much to their liking. The constrictors kill prey as large as a deer by grabbing hold with their long, curved teeth and then wrapping their bodies, which weigh up to 200 pounds, around their victim and squeezing it to death. It's not exactly what most people are looking for on their South Florida vacation.

It wouldn't be so bad if the pythons confined themselves to the Everglades, but the snakes are apparently not that great with maps. They seem to be constantly expanding their territory, though thus far none has been spotted in the state capital of Tallahassee, which is not only far to the north but is also the home of the mythical Florida Booger, which backs down to nothing, real or imagined.

Floridians might best deal with the python threat by adhering to their unofficial state motto of "Bite Back." This worked with sharks (maybe too well; some species are now threatened) and with alligators, the tails of which, when breaded and fried, make a tasty appetizer. While Python Pate may not pique too many diners' taste buds, we feel sure that our state's many wonderful and creative chefs will come up with a way to sell snake to tourists and make them think they're eating grouper.

Because if you've ever bought an acre of Florida swampland or a ticket to Disney World, you know that Florida is all about dreams and magic and places where 20-foot Burmese pythons are not only forbidden but actually unimaginable.

★ ★

The End of the Road in the Everglades
Flamingo

If Flamingo isn't the most remote spot in Florida, then what is? Even the loneliest Panhandle town lies near enough to Interstate 10 and Pensacola or Tallahassee. Even the tiniest speck of the Florida Keys clings to well-traveled U.S. Highway 1 between Miami and Key West. Even the quietest Okeechobee village joins the thickening web of country roads that crisscross central Florida.

No, this has to be it: Flamingo, population sixty-five, a tiny gateway to Florida Bay hidden deep within Everglades National Park.

Most Floridians have never heard of the place, much less visited it. They have no idea what they're missing, either, because Flamingo is at once a company town, a natural wonder, and a godforsaken haunt for mosquitoes, mosquitoes, and more mosquitoes. It's only connected to the rest of the state by a 50-mile-long park road.

"Once you get to Flamingo, you're either going by water or by foot—and not very far by foot," says Peter Allen, a park naturalist. "This is the end of the road."

Even in 1938, nine years before Everglades National Park was dedicated, naturalists realized the area lacked the popular appeal of Yellowstone or the Grand Canyon. Dan Beard, the naturalist and illustrator who is credited with bringing scouting to America in the early 1900s, noted that "There are no knife-edged mountains protruding up to the sky. There are no valleys of any kind. No glaciers exist, no gaudy canyons, no geysers, no mighty trees unless we except the few royal palms, not even a rockbound coast with the spray of ocean waves. . . . To put it crudely, there is nothing (and we include the bird rookeries) in the Everglades that will make Mr. Jonnie Q. Public suck in his breath."

This is perhaps overstated—sunsets over Florida Bay are deservedly famous—but many visitors do find the Everglades underwhelming. Still, many park rangers and workers who have lived and worked at the Grand Canyon or Yellowstone have chosen to leave the grandeur

★ ★

of those places for what is essentially a South Florida swamp.

Some Flamingoans ride their bicycles to work through "Mosquito Alley," a mangrove shortcut from employee housing to the marina. At a certain speed, mosquitoes won't land on a biker. The only problem with maintaining this speed is that large alligators sometimes lie across the path to sun themselves.

One particular gator, a sorry old three-legged fellow, has suffered many hits and near misses. He has been given a nickname: Speed Bump.

During the winter tourist season, Flamingo opens an employee pub, the Wreck Hall, where the restrooms are named Manatee and Womanatee. A weekly newsletter, *The Mullet Wrapper,* features bulletins, a humorous Mosquito Index, and the occasional employee squabble on the op-ed page. The marina store sells everything from $41 mosquito nets to 85-cent fly swatters, along with bumper stickers that read I GAVE BLOOD AT EVERGLADES NATIONAL PARK.

It would be very, very difficult to exaggerate the Flamingo mosquitoes, particularly from April through October, the rainy season. Locals know better than to venture out unprotected at dawn and dusk, lest they return with dozens of welts and bloody splotches from the suckers they've managed to swat. A common sight is a Flamingo resident out walking his dog while wearing a mosquito-proof mesh jacket complete with gloves and hood.

An equally common sight is an unsuspecting visitor performing what's known as the "Flamingo Two-Step," frantically slapping at exposed arms and legs while spraying great clouds of insect repellent.

George O'Meara, a University of Florida entomologist in Vero Beach, says Flamingo just might be the buggiest place in Florida, if not the world. For years he studied the black salt marsh mosquito (*Aedes taeniorhynchus*) and journeyed to Flamingo to collect specimens. Professionally, it was paradise. Personally, he didn't like it any more than anyone else.

"This particular mosquito, when there are billions and billions of them, they're thick even in the middle of the day," O'Meara says. "In the mangrove swamp you can hear them for a second or two when they take wing, before they engulf you. When they're bad, in the evening, you can't open your mouth if you're talking to someone.

"You have to talk through your teeth or out of the side of your mouth. If you have to take a breath or something, you'll swallow several dozen easily."

Save the Lifeguards from Their Stands!
Fort Lauderdale

In Fort Lauderdale, the city decided to replace rickety old wooden lifeguard stands with stylish new aluminum ones, to better reflect the beach community's posh image. The 2002 move was delayed, however, when officials decided the new stands were unsafe. Ramps

New doesn't always mean improved.

leading up to the towers were too steep, and lifeguards complained that side windows did not open, making them unbearably hot.

"We're not putting lifeguards in them until they are completely safe," said beach patrol lieutenant Breck Ballou.

In related news, the Fort Lauderdale Fire Department replaced fire poles with escalators to help prevent chafing. The Fort Lauderdale Sanitation Department fought to have the rear steps on garbage trucks replaced with La-Z-Boy recliners. And the Fort Lauderdale Police Department refused to wear new holsters because "they make us look fat."

Meanwhile, back at the beach, city officials have added hand railings and traction bars to the ramps. Newer stand models will have better ventilation, too, so that lifeguards will feel more comfortable. As part of a community response to the issue, Fort Lauderdale nursing homes have volunteered to help. Residents with walkers will escort lifeguards to emergencies at the water's edge, and nurse's aides will help them climb back into their stands after a rescue. New television sets with VCRs will show continuous loops of old *Baywatch* reruns.

The Old Ball Game

Fort Myers (and just about everywhere else)

If you're a baseball fan, the month of March means one thing: spring training.

The fifteen (as of this writing) major league teams that play spring-training games in Florida are known collectively as the Grapefruit League. (The counterpart in Arizona is called the Cactus League.)

Although the games are played primarily for practice and as a way to evaluate new talent, they are wildly popular with fans. More than 1.5 million tickets were sold in 2009, most of them for games played in stadiums holding fewer than 7,000 seats.

Spring training in Florida began in 1914 in St. Petersburg when former mayor, Al Lang, convinced Branch Rickey to move his St. Louis Browns to the Sunshine State for spring training. Al Lang Field,

Spring-training baseball has been played in Bradenton's McKechnie Field since 1923. Now the spring home of the Pittsburgh Pirates, the cozy 6,602-seat stadium retains its small-town charm.

recently renamed (over our objections) Progress Energy Park, sits empty now (the Tampa Bay Rays moved their spring training operations to Port Charlotte) but memories of the great baseball legends who played there— Babe Ruth, Lou Gehrig, and Mickey Mantle are just a few—remain.

Unfortunately, the small-town charm of spring training is quickly becoming a thing of the past as big, expensive stadiums replace the rickety wooden structures of yore, and ticket prices spiral.

But when it's 20 degrees in Boston and you're sitting shirtless in the Florida sun watching a ball game, things like that seem to matter less. You can find all the details about your favorite team's training schedule at www.floridagrapefruitleague.com.

Edison's Great Mind and Quirky Charm
Fort Myers

At the Thomas Edison winter home in Fort Myers, guests can walk in the famous inventor's footsteps, filing past early lightbulbs, batteries, and phonographs before learning some of the great man's quirks and charms, the gifts of an original mind.

The house Edison designed, for instance, was prefabricated in Maine before being shipped to the south bank of the Caloosahatchee River in 1886. What he called "Seminole Lodge" was practical, suited to pre-air-conditioned Florida, and had several interesting features. The electric chandeliers ("electroliers") were designed by Edison and built in his own shop. The kitchen and dining room are part of the guest house, because Edison suffered from stomach ulcers and didn't care for the smell of food cooking. Also, if his visitors proved

The Edison House in Fort Myers was prefabricated in Maine and shipped south.

tiresome, he could excuse himself after dinner and return to his own quarters, rather than having to wait for them to leave.

Edison's most famous guest was his friend and admirer Henry Ford, the automobile pioneer, who built his own winter home along the river in 1916. Both are part of the Edison-Ford Winter Estates, which offer tours every day but Christmas and Thanksgiving.

The wonders begin even before the tours start. Edison collected plants of all kinds, as part of his search for a natural source of rubber, and his friend Harvey Firestone gave him a banyan tree from Southeast Asia in 1925. That tree is now the largest banyan in North America, measuring some 400 feet across, and it's threatening to take over a museum parking lot.

A canopy of banyan trees frames a roadway in laid-back Fort Myers.

A guided tour includes what was a working research laboratory on the estate. There's a small cot where Edison, who didn't need much sleep, took catnaps during the day. After his death in 1931, workers had to test the chemicals he was using in the lab; the famous inventor, blessed with a prodigious memory, never needed to label bottles. He simply remembered what was in each one, year after year after year.

On the estate grounds, which include a friendship walk between the Ford and Edison homes, there's a swimming pool, one of the first in Florida, built with cement from Edison's cement company. Edison also had an electric boat on the river, but preferred to relax by fishing from the shore. To make sure he wasn't disturbed, he wouldn't bait his hook.

Edison was completely deaf in his later years, and one of the most personalized exhibits in the museum is a family phonograph. It has teeth marks on a wooden edge where Edison would bite down on the wood and "listen" to the music through the vibrations in his jaw.

The Edison-Ford Winter Estates, at 2350 McGregor Boulevard in Fort Myers, are open for guided tours from 9:00 a.m. to 5:30 p.m. Monday through Saturday and noon to 5:30 p.m. on Sunday, with the last tour of the day leaving at 4:00 p.m. Admission is charged. For more information visit www.edison-ford-estate.com or call (239) 334-3614.

Diamonds Are Still a Girl's Best Friend
Homestead

Edward Leedskalnin was so in love with Agnes Scuffs that he built for her a house made out of coral.

At the Coral Castle, the walls are made out of coral and the gates are made out of coral. There are coral rocking chairs, a coral bed, a coral table in the shape of a heart, coral fountains, and even a kind of coral stockade in case any children they might have (and maybe even Agnes) were ever in need of discipline.

★ ★

Edward Leedskalnin was a romantic man—he believed his fiancée would be impressed by a house made of rock.

One can only imagine what Ed would have built if he disliked Agnes.

Actually, it's all rather romantic, in a nineteenth-century Latvian sort of way. Ed was born in Latvia in 1887. When he was twenty-six, he was engaged to marry Agnes, ten years his junior. To his dying day, Ed referred to her as "Sweet Sixteen."

On the day before the wedding, Sweet Sixteen backed out on the grounds that Ed was too old for her. Ed believed there were other reasons, like the fact he had only a fourth-grade education, had no money, and enjoyed imprisoning children in coral stockades. Actually, we're making that last part up. We think.

★ ★

Anyway, Ed's heart was broken by Sweet Sixteen's rejection, so he left Latvia and spent some time wandering around Canada and the United States working at lumber camps and driving cattle.

Somehow, these itinerant occupations gave Ed the incentive, skill, and determination to single-handedly dig out, move, and arrange twenty-nine-ton slabs of coral rock into a castle of unrequited love. The work was certainly not made any easier by the fact that Ed stood 5 feet tall, weighed one hundred pounds, and was plagued with bouts of tuberculosis.

For twenty years, from 1920 to 1940, Ed worked on the home for his bride who would never be. He worked alone, at night, by lantern light, first scraping off the 2 or 3 inches of topsoil that cover the 4,000-foot-thick coral bedrock that lies beneath this part of South Florida. Then, using hand tools fashioned from parts of old Model T Fords, he chiseled, pulleyed, levered, hoisted, and dragged the mammoth slabs of fossilized coral from as far away as Florida City, 10 miles to the south.

How did Ed, a little wheezing squirt of a man with an elementary school education, assemble this 11,000-ton house, the South Florida equivalent of Stonehenge or the pyramids, all by himself? That is the essential and perhaps never-to-be-answered riddle of Coral Castle. There are no pictures, written records, or eyewitnesses to the construction. A few rotting implements in his "toolshed" are the only clues.

Ed, as you've probably surmised by now, was kind of a weird guy. Besides laboring under a Fred Flintstone–like delusion that chicks dig sleeping on beds made of rock, Ed was convinced that there are "energy lines" running between the North and South Poles that can be harnessed by six-pointed Latvian "lucky stars," several of which adorn the walls and furniture of Coral Castle.

Ed was a hermit by night but gregarious by day. He built high, thick walls to shield his work from the eyes of strangers, yet he'd let children visit during the daytime for 10 cents a head. Ed also threw in a complimentary hot dog, steamed in an old Model T differential.

⋆ ⋆

The Coral Castle story is inspiring, but also rather sad. Ed died in Miami in 1954 at the age of sixty-four. Despite repeated entreaties, the love of his life, Sweet Sixteen, never paid a single visit.

Coral Castle is located at 28655 South Dixie Highway in Homestead. Phone (305) 248-6345 or visit www.coralcastle.com. There are guided tours daily; admission is charged.

Jai-alai's Faded Glory

Miami

It's hard to believe, surveying the seedy grandeur of Miami Jai-Alai, but this game once had cachet. Beginning in the 1920s, high-society couples attended sold-out matches in dress suits and evening gowns. First Lady Eleanor Roosevelt attended a performance, and later on the matches were shown on local television. The Miami arena, or fronton, was known as "The Yankee Stadium of Jai-alai."

Today the game remains the same, a fascinating cultural artifact from the Basque region of Spain, but the scene has changed.

The Miami fronton is now located in the industrial park limbo that is "near the airport." It's the kind of place where you park in the lot, and then double-check to make sure your doors are locked. Inside, the stands reek of cigarette smoke, most of the seats are empty, and it's the rare leaping play that draws approving calls from the crowd. More common is energetic, multilingual cussing when bettors play their hunches and lose, or when a lucky number fails to fall into place.

Still, the place has a certain down-at-the-heels charm, and it might be the perfect antidote to a day at Disney World.

Jai-alai—pronounced *high-lie* (it means "merry festival" in Basque)—certainly is different, practically unique to Florida in the United States. Five of the nation's six frontons are here, in Dania, Fort Pierce, Ocala, Orlando, and Miami. The Miami arena is the largest, with 6,000 seats, and the oldest, built in 1926. It features American and Basque players who go by marvelous one-word names such as Areitio, Lejardi, and

★ ★

Zumaya. When a game comes down to the final point, and fans are shouting out encouragement, the fronton doesn't seem so jaded.

The sport is sometimes billed as "the world's fastest game," because players can hurl a ball, or pelota, at speeds greater than 150 miles per hour. Jai-alai is played on a three-sided court, and players must use a curved basket, or cesta, to catch the ball and fling it back against the front wall in one fluid motion.

It's a little like racquetball, only much cooler.

Because most fans are more interested in gambling than in the game itself, the state lottery has hurt attendance and forced several frontons out of business. Today the fronton offers large-screen televisions so gamblers can follow their bets on everything from football to Thoroughbred and harness racing.

It's hard to believe the game will rebound and regain its former glory, but who knows? It's a long shot, but so is winning a superfecta bet, and jai-alai fans take those odds every day.

Miami Jai-Alai is located at 3500 N.W. 37th Avenue. Call (305) 633-6400 for match times.

Cracking Good Claws
Miami Beach

If it's a relaxing, romantic evening you're looking for, Joe's Stone Crab restaurant is probably not the place for you.

A Miami Beach institution since 1913, Joe's atmosphere can best be described as . . . pandemonium. The restaurant's 400 seats are always full during stone crab season (October 15–May 15), and the wait for a table can sometimes take two hours. Or more. No reservations are accepted at Joe's; you line up with everyone else and wait your turn.

But if you love stone crab claws (and who doesn't?), the wait is worth it. The hard-shelled claws come pre-cracked, so all you have to do is dip them into Joe's equally famous mustard sauce and enjoy. Steaks and other seafood dishes are available, but if you're not coming to Joe's for stone crab claws, it hardly seems worth the bother.

★ ★

Seminole Statement of 1936

After more than a century of war, deprivation, and relocation to reservations, the Seminoles of Florida wanted no part of dealing with the United States of America. In 1936, state officials organized a Seminole Conference near Monroe Station in the Everglades east of Naples. Tribal spokesmen were wary, though, and told the governor they wanted only one thing. "Pohoan chekish," they said. Leave us alone.

(Hint: Leave plenty of ceiling on your credit card; these claws come with lobster-esque price tags.)

Joe Weiss, a Hungarian immigrant, started Joe's as a lunch stand next to Smith's bathing casino. Joe's specialty was fish sandwiches until a local ichthyologist urged him to boil up some stone crabs, a prevalent but widely ignored denizen of the local bays. The claws (the only edible part of the crab) were an instant hit, and Joe's restaurant soon became a local landmark. Over the years, everyone who is anyone has dined at Joe's: Al Capone, Will Rogers, Amelia Earhart, the Duke and Duchess of Windsor, and J. Edgar Hoover (presumably not while Scarface was in the building). More recently, former President Bill Clinton dined at Joe's. (He reportedly ordered the fried chicken.)

Taking up an entire city block, Joe's is located in the heart of Miami Beach's flamboyant nightclub district, so people-watching can occupy your time between bites of stone crab.

Dinner at Joe's is pretty much a must for anyone visiting South Florida for the first time. But don't go if you're in a hurry; restaurants over ninety years old are entitled to move at their own pace.

Joe's Stone Crab restaurant is located at 11 Washington Avenue in Miami Beach. Phone (305) 673-0365 or go online at www.joesstone crab.com.

The Middle of Everything
North Miami Beach

It's a lonely road to Florida state parks. They're in between towns, for the most part, with few conveniences. If you want wine, movies, or Chee-tos, you better bring them with you. Then there's Oleta River State Park in North Miami Beach. When you go there for a visit, you're not exactly getting away from it all. More like driving into the middle of everything.

Oleta River is a traffic jam stuck in the dregs of East Coast sprawl between Miami and Fort Lauderdale. Condos and office buildings rise in every direction. It doesn't even get dark at night, because there's so much ambient light surrounding the place.

Call it urban camping.

If you get the munchies, there's every restaurant chain and fast food franchise known to man. Krispy Kreme for breakfast? Look for the HOT NOW sign. Big Mac for lunch? Arches all over the place. Chili's for dinner? Happy hour starts at 4:00 p.m. If you want shopping, there's something for everyone. The highways are lined with discount shops and outlet stores. Dwarfing them all is the Aventura Mall, where it's quite a hike from Macy's to Bloomingdale's.

And if you want a lap dance, well, there's not one but two strip clubs within five minutes of the park gates.

In other words, Oleta River isn't the usual Florida outdoor experience. The North Miami Beach state park is good for two things, though—mangrove paddling and mountain biking.

Florida kayakers take the scenery for granted, but newcomers love paddling along the mangroves. Sometimes those mangroves form a canopy over a canoe trail. Sometimes fiddler crabs swarm all over that canopy. Sometimes people find that spooky. Dade and Broward

County mountain bikers have carved out an impressive number of trails in the 1,000-acre state park. Expert paths will scare the bejesus out of all but the most experienced and enthusiastic riders. They carry names such as El Diablo, Rocky Mile, and Gates of Delirium.

After pedaling and paddling—or shopping and sightseeing—it's time to rest.

Oleta River log cabins are handsome enough, but spectacularly ill-suited for south Florida. With few windows and little ventilation, you pretty much have to use the little wall air conditioners, which makes it feel like a motel room. In a way, that's what it is, an inexpensive place to stay when visiting Miami and Fort Lauderdale.

It's easy to forget you're in a Florida state park.

Oleta River State Park, 3400 N.E. 163rd Street, North Miami, is open from 8:00 a.m. to dusk daily. It offers biking, paddling, swimming, and picnicking. For more information call (305) 919-1846.

The Country's Smallest Post Office

Ochopee

Tiny, buggy Ochopee, which is hardly a bump on a road in the Everglades, has become a pilgrimage of sorts for philatelists from across the country and around the world. Stamp collectors, you see, crave letters with a postmark from what's believed to be the nation's smallest post office.

It's hard to imagine a smaller one, because the Ochopee Post Office looks little bigger than an outhouse. Considering the time-honored use of the Sears catalog, and the modern proliferation of junk mail, this may be considered social commentary.

The tin-roofed and white-painted hut sits on a curve in US 41, the old Tamiami Trail highway, about an hour southeast of Naples. There's a flagpole to one side of the building, and a picnic table to the other, with a gravel parking lot for cars to circle. A green historical marker, which is almost bigger than the office itself, explains the history of the place.

When Asked, Just Say It Tastes Like Chicken

It is illegal to feed Florida alligators, but it's not illegal for them to feed us.

Farm-raised alligators not only provide hides for pricey belts and handbags, they also produce a tasty white meat that is low in fat and high in protein. Most Florida crackers prefer to deep fry their gator meat, most of which comes from the animal's tail, but barbecued gator ribs also occasionally show up on the dinner plate.

If you don't happen to have a gator farm near you, the best way to obtain this white and somewhat chewy meat is over the Internet. Orlando-based Gatorland, the self-proclaimed "Alligator Capital of the World," not only has plenty of gator-related exhibits, it also sells gator meat. Visit the park or go to www.gatorland.com for more information.

In any case, here's a rather typical recipe for fried alligator tail, courtesy of Ken Nipper of www.recipezaar.com:

2 lbs. alligator tail (steaks or chunks)
¼ teaspoon salt
¼ teaspoon pepper
¼ teaspoon garlic powder
¼ teaspoon onion powder
¼ cup powdered milk
½ cup flour
2 cups cornmeal
Oil for deep frying. (Peanut is best.)

1. Salt and pepper alligator meat, then set aside.

2. Mix flour, corn meal, salt, pepper, garlic powder, onion powder and powdered milk.

3. Heat oil to about 400 degrees F. in deep fryer. Dredge gator pieces in flour mixture and fry for 3 to 5 minutes or until brown. Overcooking will toughen the meat.

4. Drain cooked pieces on paper towels. Serve with favorite dipping sauce. Serves 4.

It seems that the building was once an irrigation pipe shed for the J. T. Gaunt Company tomato farm. After a night fire burned down the old Ochopee general store and post office in 1953, the shed was pressed into service by postmaster Sidney Brown. It's been in use ever since, still serving local families and the stamp fans who drop off mail to collect postmarks.

UPS and Federal Express, presumably, aren't interested in challenging this monopoly.

"Nude Everglades" Gallery
Ochopee

Visitors to Ochopee tend to stop across the street from the Smallest Post Office to visit Joanie's Blue Crab Cafe, which is becoming an attraction in its own right.

The timeworn cafe dates back to the 1930s, when it was a storage building for the Standard service station next door. Now the gas station is closed, and the shed offers snacks, meals, and restrooms "for patrons only." The musty place is filled with souvenirs, paintings for sale, and poetry for everyone to share:

Mosquito, mosquito, why do you sting?
Such a big pain, from a little thing!
Mosquito, mosquito, I can get you with a smack,
But your billions of relatives keep coming back!

You can read other such poems in one of the Blue Crab's restrooms. The other restroom is less literary and more, um, graphic. Its walls are covered with framed photographs of half-nekkid local women posed outdoors. A few of them wear thongs at the beach, or embrace pickup trucks, while another is draped only in a Confederate flag.

Southern soft-core. Skeeter porn. Playglades.

When asked about this gallery, the store manager laughs and explains that it's part of the "Nude Everglades" portfolio of an Ochopee amateur photographer. This guy takes pictures of his wife and other local women, and goes by the name "Lucky."

Well, he'd have to be.

Joanie's Blue Crab Cafe can be found at 39395 Tamiami Trail, Ochopee. It's open from 11:00 a.m. to 5:00 p.m. in summer and 11:00 a.m. to 8:00 p.m. in winter. It's a good idea to call first and check on the hours. Depending on how busy they are, the cafe sometimes closes sooner or later than its official hours. Phone (239) 695-2682.

Arabian Nights
Opa-Locka

Entering the city of Opa-Locka in northern Miami-Dade County is like stepping through the pages of *1001 Arabian Nights.*

The entire city, founded in 1926, is done up in a Moorish theme. Everywhere you turn you'll see domes, parapets, minarets, and key-hole arches. Opa-Locka City Hall, located on Sharazad Boulevard, looks like an elaborate Persian palace. With more than eighty themed buildings still standing, Opa-Locka claims the largest collection of Moorish architecture in the Western Hemisphere. Twenty of the buildings are on the National Register of Historic Places.

Opa-Locka was the brainchild of Glenn H. Curtiss, a brilliant engineer and inventor from New York. (Curtiss was quite a story himself. He was featured on the cover of *Time* magazine in 1924 and has been declared the "Father of Naval Aviation.") Like many others, Curtiss came to Florida in the 1920s to speculate in real estate. He wound up founding several South Florida cities, including Hialeah, Miami Springs, and Coral Gables.

But it's Opa-Locka that causes people to stop, scratch their heads, and go, "Huh?"

Apparently, Curtiss was just ga-ga over the book *1001 Arabian Nights,* especially the descriptions of the ornate architecture. So he thought he'd build a little Morocco right here in the Florida swamp. (The Tequesta Indian name for the place is *Opatishawockalocka,* which means "big swamp." Curtiss wisely shortened the name to Opa-Locka.)

Curtiss hired German architect Bernhard Muller to design the city. A hotel, zoo, train station, and airport were completed before the land boom went bust and work stopped.

Today, new buildings have to comply with the Moorish theme. There aren't many new buildings, however; downtown Opa-Locka is plagued by crime and drugs.

But in its day, Opa-Locka was a place even a sultan would admire.

Where the Other Half Stays
Palm Beach

In 1904, a room at The Breakers started at $4 a night. Expensive, yes, but keep in mind that that included three meals a day.

Today, the cheapest room in the palatial Palm Beach hotel goes for $320 a night. (If you have to ask what the most expensive room goes for, you can't afford it.)

Like so much of the east coast of Florida, The Breakers can attribute its existence to the redoubtable Henry Flagler. A Standard Oil magnate, Flagler built a system of railroads on the East Coast, opening up that part of Florida to tourism and development.

Presumably so he'd have a nice place to stay while counting his money, Flagler in 1894 built the first hotel on the southeast coast of Florida, The Royal Poinciana. Built in Lake Worth, the hotel quickly began drawing the rich and famous to what would become Palm Beach.

In 1896, Flagler built a second hotel, the Palm Beach Inn, next to the Royal Poinciana but closer to the ocean. Guests were soon requesting rooms "by the breakers." When the Palm Beach Inn was expanded, Flagler renamed it The Breakers.

Fire destroyed the hotel twice. The hotel that stands today opened in 1927 and is as much an art gallery as a place for people to eat and sleep. Modeled after the Villa Medici in Rome, The Breakers has hand-painted ceilings in its 200-foot-long lobby and public rooms. The painting and ornamentation were done by seventy-five artists shipped in from Italy.

The hotel is enormous, with 560 rooms and a staff of 1,800. There is an eighteen-hole golf course on the hotel grounds and also a 20,000-square-foot spa overlooking the ocean.

Dinner in the elegant L'Escalier restaurant is, unfortunately, not included in the price of your room.

For more information visit online at www.thebreakers.com or call (561) 655-6611.

The Shell Factory and "The Sanibel Stoop"
Sanibel Island

If you look at a map of Florida's Gulf Coast, you'll notice that most of the coastal keys are long, thin islands that follow the shoreline north and south. The exception to that rule is Lee County's Sanibel Island, which is an east-west crescent swinging out into the Gulf of Mexico.

That's why there are so many seashells on the island, especially after tropical storms move up the coast. The popular island sport is called "shelling" by locals and tourists alike, and there's even a name for the position assumed by so many shellers: "The Sanibel Stoop."

Local shell history and literary notables include Anne Morrow Lindbergh, wife of the famous aviator and author of *Gift from the Sea,* the 1955 bestseller. She wrote the book on Captiva Island, which extends north of Sanibel. *Gift from the Sea* uses different seashells as a launching point for meditations on love and marriage, peace and happiness.

Today, on the mainland of Lee County, in North Fort Myers, there's the profoundly unmeditative Shell Factory, where nautical treasures meet the mass market of tourism. In this 75,000-square-foot complex, thousands of samples of thousands of seashells fill yard after yard of exhibit space. There are common and rare shells, ranging from *Telescopium* (3 for $1) to *Cypraea valentia* ($4,000 apiece). Only 5

★ ★

percent of the inventory is domestic, with the rest coming from fifty countries around the globe.

Souvenirs include shell-encrusted novelties, dolls, and lamps made in Taiwan and the Philippines. Then there are beach towels, snorkels, and the usual Florida bric-a-brac, along with a growing section of Christmas decorations and novelties. Finally, for when families are shelled and shopped out, there are concessions, wildlife exhibits, and bumper boat rides.

By then they'll be ready to return to the quiet shelling of Sanibel Island.

The Shell Factory is at 2787 North Tamiami Trail in North Fort Myers. Hours are 9:00 a.m. to 9:00 p.m. Monday through Saturday, 9:00 a.m. to 8:00 p.m. Sunday. Call (239) 995-2141 for more information.

Who Put the "Ding" in Ding Darling?
Sanibel Island

Birders know the call, and its meaning, but tourists might be forgiven for assuming that the words *Ding Darling* announce cocktail hour at exclusive resorts on the Florida Gulf Coast.

Even locals might be surprised to learn that J. N. "Ding" Darling, namesake of the National Wildlife Refuge on Sanibel Island, began his career with a poison pen. His political cartoons won two Pulitzer Prizes and appeared in more than 150 newspapers in the early 1900s. Later on he became better known as a sportsman and conservationist, the founder of the National Wildlife Federation, and a pioneer who fought for the preservation of habitat throughout Florida.

If all this information isn't enough to win bar bets and trivia contests, go with this one: Darling was known as "Ding" to everyone, but the J. N. stood for Jay Norwood.

The J. N. "Ding" Darling National Wildlife Refuge is at One Wildlife Drive, off Sanibel-Captiva Road. Visitor center hours are 9:00 a.m. to 5:00 p.m. An entrance fee is charged. For more information call (239) 472-1100.

★ ★

Florida's Hippest Beach
South Beach

South Beach wasn't always the swingin' place that it is today.

In the 1870s, the southern portion of Miami Beach between 1st and 23rd Streets was a coconut grove. Some people would argue that the place has gone downhill since then, but that is only their opinion. Even if we can't stay up late enough to partake in all the pleasures South Beach has to offer, we appreciate a place where the nightclubs don't really start to rock until 3:00 a.m. and slinky European models tend to forget their bikini tops.

South Beach has been many things over the years and few of them could be described as hip or sophisticated. In the 1980s, the place was more popular with Cuban cocaine dealers than it was with tourists. The TV show *Miami Vice* was filmed here and did a lot to shape South Beach's image as a dangerous, decadent but terrifically exciting place. Before that, South Beach was a slowly decaying retirement village favored by Jews from New York. In the 1930s, this group of transplants built some of the smaller art deco hotels along lower Collins Avenue and Ocean Drive. Today, that distinctive form of retro architecture is as much a part of South Beach as its ocean vistas and cultural diversity. (As of 2000, 55 percent of Miami Beach residents, which includes South Beach, spoke Spanish as their first language.)

The luminous stretch of sand that is South Beach drew the attention of the fashion industry in the late 1980s and soon it was a preferred backdrop for some of the world's most famous fashion photographers—and models.

So people-watching is probably the number one diversion on South Beach, followed closely by nightclub-hopping and sun-tanning.

As you soak in the scene—and the rays—try to picture the place as a coconut grove.

A few margaritas can only help.

* *

The World's Largest Drive-In

Sunrise

There are thirty-two outdoor movie screens in Florida, and more than a third of them are at the Thunderbird Drive-In near Fort Lauderdale. It's the mother of all drive-ins, the largest in the United States, and a big fat slice of Americana. If drive-ins are dinosaurs, a dying breed, then the Thunderbird is *Jurassic Park*—and *Jurassic Park II* and *Jurassic Park III.*

The Thunderbird is no nostalgia house catering to aging baby boomers, though. It's more of a gritty outdoor multiplex doing bulk business in a seedy neighborhood. By day, it's a parking lot lined with stalls for the huge Swap Shop flea market, which offers both an on-site McDonald's and the Daily Circus. At night the space is cleared for cars and moviegoers.

The Thunderbird keeps adding screens—thirteen at the latest count. It is by all accounts the largest drive-in theater in the country, and probably in the world. This is true even though the place opened inauspiciously on November 22, 1963, the day John F. Kennedy was assassinated.

Even today, the Thunderbird is a little unbelievable, and unexpected, for many tourists.

When Florida visitor John Savage was growing up in New Hampshire, he went to drive-in movies with his parents—everything from *The Great Escape* to *The Dirty Dozen.* On vacation in Fort Lauderdale, he decided to take his wife and four kids to an old-fashioned drive-in. They found the Thunderbird in the phone book.

"When we called and they started reading off the list of movies, we said, 'Oh, this can't be a drive-in,'" Savage says. "But it is."

From any one Thunderbird movie, you can glimpse the screens for three or four others. Free previews are fine, of course, but not at the wrong moment. When the dramatic *Black Hawk Down* debuted

★ ★

in 2002, it was hard not to be distracted by Britney Spears dancing around in her underwear for *Crossroads* on the next screen.

The Thunderbird Drive-In is at the Swap Shop flea market—you can't miss it—at 3291 W. Sunrise Boulevard in Sunrise. For more information call (954) 791-7927.

5

The Florida Keys

Compared to the *hulking peninsula of Florida to the north, the Keys seem like an afterthought, a flimsy comma of islands and islets that improbably manage to separate the Atlantic Ocean from the Gulf of Mexico.*

You don't just stumble upon the Keys; you have to really want to go there. The drive down US 1 is a bear, what with traffic and the seemingly endless succession of bridges. And the distances are not insignificant, either. Lots of people headed to Key West think they've broken the back of the trip once they reach Miami. All too quickly they learn that they still have 154 miles to go, a trip of 3½ hours if traffic is moving freely, which it seldom is. By contrast, Key West is only 90 miles from Havana. Back in the 1980s, the mayor of Key West water-skied to Havana in a little less than six hours. He didn't give a reason; he just felt like doing it—which pretty much reflects a Key Wester's attitude toward life in general.

It's this kind of vibe that attracts people to the Keys. There's also great fishing, snorkeling and diving opportunities, particularly at John Pennekamp Coral Reef State Park (www.pennekamppark.com) on Key Largo. Most tourists head to Key West, the last island in the chain and the southernmost point in the United States. (We know this is true because it says so right there on the thermos-bottle-shaped thingy at the corner of South Street and Whitehead Street.) It's a compact town, Key West, so you really don't need to drive. You can see the sights by walking, renting

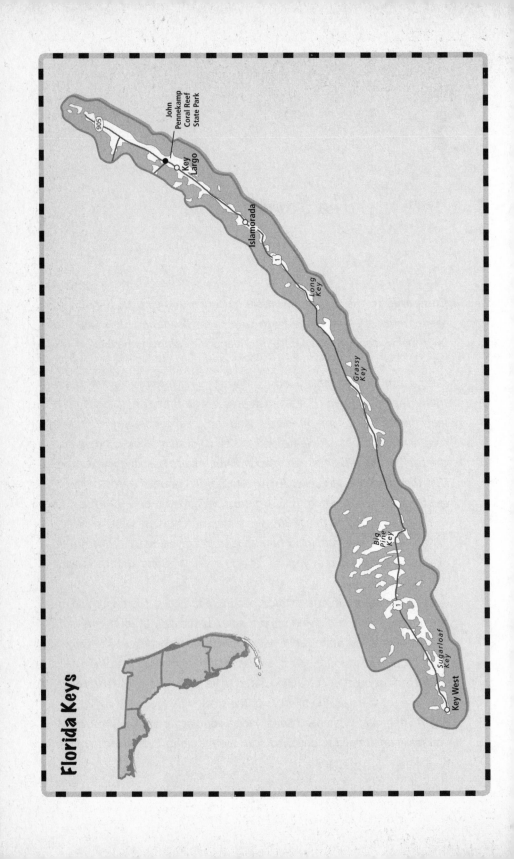

Florida Keys

John
Pennekamp
Coral Reef
State Park

905

Key
Largo

Islamorada

Long
Key

Grassy
Key

Big
Pine
Key

Sugarloaf
Key

Key West

a bike or riding in the back of one of the quirky pedal cabs. Though bar-hopping is a favorite pastime in Key West, there are other things to do as well. A guided tour of the Hemingway House (www.hemingway home.com) is a must. You'll hear the story of the six-toed cats and construction of the swimming pool, the first on the Key.

If that's not enough Hemingway for you for one day, meander over to Sloppy Joe's Bar at 201 Duval Street (www.sloppyjoes.com), one of several watering holes frequented by Papa and his buddies during the 1930s.

Who knows, after a few Sloppy Ritas you might even get the urge to write the Great American Novel. Or, you can simply wobble back to your hotel for a restorative nap.

PHOTO COURTESY OF VISIT FLORIDA

Honey, I Shrunk the Deer
Big Pine Key

Bambi is alive and well and living on Big Pine Key.

The pine forests of this largely undeveloped island are home to most of the world's population of Key deer. Looking more like a medium-sized dog than a deer, an adult Key deer might weigh only forty-five pounds and stand only 25 inches tall at the shoulder.

Needless to say, these little guys are adorably cute to the point that you just want to scoop one up in your arms and take him home with you. That, of course, would be a big mistake. Key deer are a protected species; take all the photos you want but don't try to feed them, pet them, or cuddle them.

All of the Key deer in the world live in Monroe County. The smallest North American deer, they're the diminutive cousins of the Virginia white-tailed deer and are believed to have become stranded on the Keys thousands of years ago when rising water cut off their access to the mainland.

Once hunted with dogs nearly to the point of extinction, Key deer now number in the 250 to 300 range. Stray dogs still kill a few of these little guys every year. Loss of habitat and traffic on busy US 1 are also threats.

The best place to see a Key deer is at the National Key Deer Refuge on Big Pine Key. The fawn-colored animals are most active in the morning and evening, but chances are good that you'll see one any time of day.

It's like watching a Disney animated feature—only without all the annoying previews.

For more information on National Key Deer Refuge, call (305) 872-2239.

★ ★

The Importance of Tail-Walking

Grassy Key

Dolphins (and their porpoise cousins) are abundant in the warm coastal waters of Florida, but it's still a thrill to tourists and residents alike when the sleek mammals are spotted playing in the wake of a boat or simply gliding along.

Of all the thousands of dolphins, one was singled out for everlasting fame. That dolphin is, of course, Flipper. Star of the 1963 movie (costarring Chuck Connors), Flipper's real name was Mitzi. Mitzi (yes, Flipper was a she, not a he) was trained, and the movie shot, at what is now the Dolphin Research Center at Mile Marker 59 on Grassy Key. Back in the early '60s, the DRC was called Santini's Porpoise School. It was run by Milton Santini, a pioneer in dolphin training. Mitzi was Santini's first (and obviously most famous) pupil and became the star of the movie and the subsequent TV series, which ran from 1964 to 1967.

Although most of the stunts, such as towing damaged boats to shore and whacking guns out of bad guys' hands with her nose or tail, were performed by Mitzi, the tail-walking scenes were done by a "stunt double" dolphin by the name of Mr. Gipper. (Mitzi never mastered tail-walking; perhaps she deemed it unladylike.)

Mitzi died of a heart attack in 1972 and was buried beneath a dolphin statue in the school's courtyard. The 30-foot concrete statue of a mother and baby dolphin is now maintained by the DRC, an organization devoted to research and dolphin awareness.

A plaque beneath the statue reads:

DEDICATED TO THE MEMORY OF MITZI
THE ORIGINAL FLIPPER
1958–1972

Mitzi had no offspring, but Mr. Gipper did. His daughter, Tursy, is reported to be a fine tail-walker.

★ ★

Robbie's School of Tarpon
Islamorada

Robbie's Marina in Islamorada sells bait and rents kayaks, but the main attraction swims beneath the docks. They're tarpon—big ones, and lots of them—and they school outside the marina like giant silver sardines. For anglers who know tarpon as fierce saltwater game fish, this is curious indeed—imagine a pride of lions lining up to be fed like a cuddle of kittens.

The story goes that an injured tarpon named Scarface was rehabilitated at Robbie's in 1976, and it kept returning to the dock. Soon there were dozens of tarpon, scores of them, all waiting to be fed. They show up in the morning and leave in the evening, unless there's really cold weather or really rough seas.

Some 50,000 people visit Robbie's each year; the more notable visitors have included tennis star Chris Evert and former Vice President Al Gore.

For $1, guests get a pail of herring—tiny ones—to feed to the tarpon. The huge fish mill around the docks and will even rise out of the water to grab a bite. Above the docks, it gets just as crowded.

"Oh, we're jammed all the time," said Joe Saba, a backcountry guide at Robbie's. "We opened at eight this morning, and I've already sold 200 pounds of bait."

Robbie's Marina is at Mile Marker 77 under the Lignumvitae Bridge in Islamorada. Phone (305) 664-9814.

Undersea Lodging, à la Jules Verne
Key Largo

The Jules Verne–inspired Jules' Undersea Lodge may be the only underwater hotel in the world, but it's hardly 20,000 Leagues Under the Sea. The submersible doesn't move, and there's no mad captain bent on taking over the world. As a former NASA research vessel, it's more science fact than fiction.

Then again, the place was featured on the old television show

★ ★

Lifestyles of the Rich and Famous, and host Robin Leach could be pretty frightening.

The unique lodge, which opened in 1986, is a mere 21 feet beneath the surface of Emerald Lagoon in Key Largo. Guests pay more than $300 a night to dive into the hotel, entering through a wet room before enjoying two bedrooms, a bathroom, and a living room, along with huge round windows that offer a stunning view of surrounding marine life.

Talk about sleeping with the fishes.

The Undersea Lodge isn't exactly spacious, or luxurious, but it does offer some amenities. These include hot showers, air-conditioning, and televisions with VCRs. If guests order the lodge luxury package, a "mer-chef" will see to a gourmet meal. For more casual meals, there's underwater delivery from a local pizza shop.

The lodge is filled with compressed air, and a soft bubbling sound is said to offer a fine night's sleep—if guests aren't suffering from Jules Vernian nightmares.

Those round lodge windows, some 42 inches in diameter, feature parading schools of angelfish and parrot fish, along with less colorful but more exciting barracuda. NASA originally used the laboratory vessel, known as *La Chalupa*—really, no kidding—off the continental shelf near Puerto Rico. The idea was to explore the similarities and differences between life underwater and life in outer space.

Guests today can explore the area around the lodge without heavy diving equipment. Instead, they use 100-foot "hookah" breathing lines left over from the days of research. Nearby is Marine Lab, an underwater facility devoted to research and education, along with a re-creation of a Spanish galleon wreck. The lodge offers hours of what is called habitat saturation diving, but guests don't have to have any scuba experience at all.

Jules' Undersea Lodge offers a three-hour class to acquaint noncertified divers with the equipment and procedures necessary to descend to the lodge, accompanied by diving instructors.

* *

PHOTO COURTESY OF VISIT FLORIDA

The lodge is monitored by a command center at the edge of the lagoon. An umbilical cable provides fresh air, drinking water, electricity, and telephone lines. Two couples or a group of six friends may share the lodge, but there are honeymoon packages available. Celebrity guests have included former Canadian prime minister Pierre Trudeau and Steven Tyler of the rock band Aerosmith.

Jules' Undersea Lodge is at Key Largo Undersea Park, 51 Shoreland Drive in Key Largo. For more information visit www.jul.com or call (305) 451-2353.

The Name "Tourist Trap" Must Have Already Been Taken

Why are the Florida Keys called the Keys? Don't blame Ponce de León, he of Fountain of Youth fame. The explorer, who apparently suffered from a much too vivid imagination, decided after seeing the chain of islands on the horizon for the first time that they looked like men who were suffering. (Remember, this was way before wives started dragging their husbands to gift shops.) He gave the islands the name "Los Martires," or "the martyrs."

Perhaps realizing that future chambers of commerce would have trouble warming up to the slogan "Be a Martyr! Visit Martyr West!" the chain was eventually renamed "keys" from the Spanish *cayos*, meaning "small islands."

So today we have Key Largo and Marathon Key and Big Pine Key, but no Martyr Key. Which is probably a good thing.

Underwater Park and Christ of the Deep

Key Largo

For a mainland visitor to the Florida Keys, it's hard to say which is more impressive, the colors of the coral reefs along Key Largo or the clarity of the water surrounding them. On a clear day, it's like swimming through an enormous saltwater aquarium.

Rainbow parrot fish dart about in brilliant purple and teal. Vivid green moray eels lurk along the bottom. Bright blue tangs join elegant angelfish and schools of French grunts, all yellow and striped. In less than an hour, you'll see more kinds of tropical fish than you can count, along with plenty of barracuda and sharks. Then there's all the coral: brain coral and staghorn coral, pillar coral and ribbon coral, ivory tube coral and orange tube coral. Finally, if you're lucky, a huge spotted eagle ray, some 7 feet across, will glide along the bottom with effortless grace.

It's small wonder, then, that this area is protected as both the Florida Keys National Marine Sanctuary and John Pennekamp Coral Reef State Park.

The Key Largo coral reefs are remarkable for being both beautiful and accessible. One of their most appealing attributes doesn't seem that important until visitors arrive in Key Largo: They're shallow. Many of the reefs are only 5, 10, or 20 feet below the surface. This means snorkelers can enjoy them just as much as scuba divers can.

"In some parts of the world, reefs are more of a diver's thing," says Danny Jones, manager of the state park. "Novice snorkelers can go to any of the reefs around here."

Often snorkeling is less of a sport than a leisure activity. With swim fins and an inflatable dive vest to keep you afloat, hardly any effort is required. "If you're jetting around, you'll scare the marine life, anyway," says Nestor Morales, a dive master out of Biscayne National Park. "I tell people, 'The slower you go, the more you'll see. Take it easy out there.'"

Looming over the reef known as Dry Rocks is the *Christ of the Deep* statue. It's a 9-foot-high, 4,000-pound bronze piece, built in 1961, that was modeled after *Il Christo Degli Abissi*, "Christ of the Abysses," near Genoa, Italy. Divers who happen to be atheists don't care for the statue, and have protested against it, but it's become part of the local seascape.

Even though snorkelers swim among eels, barracudas, and nurse sharks, incidents and injuries are rare. They're much more likely to get sunburned or dehydrated. The danger people pose to the reefs, however, is very real. It takes hundreds of years for a piece of coral to grow, but a careless or thoughtless snorkeler can snap off a piece in a second.

★ ★

"It's a hands-off environment," Morales says. "There's a saying: Don't touch it, don't take it, don't break it." Reefs can get crowded, but the human impact on the coral is slight so long as swimmers keep their hands and fins to themselves.

There are many private tour and dive boat operators in the Florida Keys. John Pennekamp Coral Reef State Park offers dive, snorkel, and glass-bottom boat tours out of Key Largo. Call (305) 451–1202 for information. To the north, Biscayne National Park offers snorkeling trips out of Homestead. Call (305) 230-1100 for information.

Chicken of the Sea
Key West

Visitors to Key West may be surprised to see an abundance of free-range chickens roaming the streets and yards of the island resort.

The abundant, free-range "gypsy" chickens of Key West are a big hit among tourists. With the locals, not so much.

Key West or Bust!

If you look to the west of the beautiful Seven Mile Bridge, which connects Marathon and Little Duck Keys, you will see what looks like an ultralong fishing pier. Besides the fishermen, there are bicyclists, joggers, walkers, and people just out to enjoy the view. What they may not be aware of as they gaze over the turquoise Gulf of Mexico is that they are standing on all that's left of the Eighth Wonder of the World, or Flagler's Folly, as it was referred to by less charitable sorts.

Henry Flagler, an oil baron and railroad tycoon (he built the first railroad connecting Jacksonville to Miami, which explains why there is a county in northeast Florida named after him), decided in 1904, at the age of seventy-five, that he wanted to build a railroad connecting Miami to Key West. Some say he wanted to do business with Cuba, only 90 miles to the south. Others say the fortune he amassed from Standard Oil left him feeling guilty and he wanted to give something back to the people. (We tend to go with the first explanation.)

No matter the reason behind it, the fact that there ever was such a thing as the Overseas Railroad is, to say the least, remarkable. The northern part of the railroad, from Homestead to Key Largo, had to be built in the Everglades, where heavy machinery sank in the muck. Between the mosquitoes, the snakes, and the alligators, few workers stayed on the job long.

The railway, which was more than 100 miles long, ran along 20 miles of man-made causeways and over 12 miles of bridges, of which the Seven Mile Bridge was the longest. The engineering challenges would have been immense even without the two hurricanes that barreled through the Keys during construction, resulting in loss of life, major equipment damage, and second thoughts about whether the whole project was worth it.

But Flagler, his health failing, never gave up, and kept pouring money into the project. "Go to Key West!" he exhorted his engineers after every setback.

The railroad finally opened for business on January 22, 1912. Henry Flagler rode the first train from Miami to Key West, where he was joyously welcomed by the 17,000 residents of the island that the day before had been accessible only by boat. New Yorkers could now board a Pullman in Penn Station and not get out until they hit Havana. (The Pullmans were loaded onto ferries in Key West for the 90-mile trip to Cuba.)

The Overseas Railroad didn't just cater to swells, however. A round-trip ticket from Miami to Key West cost $4.75. If you could wait until Sunday, the ticket price was only $2.50.

But as wondrous as it was, the Overseas Railroad never made a profit. What the Great Depression started, the Labor Day Hurricane of 1935 finished. The most violent storm in American history, the hurricane's 250-miles-per-hour wind gusts and 18-foot storm surge irreparably damaged the railroad, and Flagler sold what was left to the State of Florida.

Three years later, the railroad reopened as a two-lane highway, the remnants of which are what you're really looking at from the new bridge. The tracks were torn up and fashioned into guardrails. With each lane only about 5 feet wide, truck drivers were instructed at the beginning of Seven Mile Bridge to pull their outside mirrors in to avoid clipping oncoming vehicles.

What if you broke down on your way to Key West and needed to pull off on the shoulder? Plenty of room: To the right was the Gulf of Mexico and to the left was the Atlantic Ocean.

Finding a mechanic on the bottom of the sea, however, was another matter.

Stop at Pigeon Key, Mile Marker 47, for a good view of the old Overseas Railroad. The key was once a camp for railroad workers. A visitor center on the east side of the island is a good place to learn more about the history of Flagler's Folly.

Key Lime Pie Recipe

Here is a basic recipe for Key lime pie, courtesy of Joe's Stone Crab restaurant:

1 cup plus 2 tablespoons graham-cracker crumbs
5 tablespoons unsalted butter, melted
⅓ cup sugar
3 egg yolks
1 teaspoon grated lime zest
1 (14 ounces) can sweetened condensed milk
⅔ cup fresh Key lime juice
1 cup heavy cream
3 tablespoons confectioner's sugar

1. Preheat oven to 350 degrees.

2. In a large mixing bowl, combine graham crackers, butter, and sugar. Press mixture into bottom and sides of a buttered 9-inch pan, forming a neat border around edge.

3. Bake crust about 5 minutes or until set and golden.

4. Using an electric mixer with a whisk attachment and a non-reactive bowl, beat egg yolks and lime zest at high speed about 5 minutes or until very shiny. Gradually add condensed milk and continue to beat 3 to 4 minutes or until thick. Reduce speed of mixer to low. Add lime juice and mix until just combined. Pour lime mixture into crust.

5. Bake about 10 minutes or until filling has just set. Cool to room temperature, then refrigerate.

6. To serve, place pie in freezer for 15 to 20 minutes before serving. In an electric mixer bowl, combine cream and confectioner's sugar. Whisk until nearly stiff. Cut pie into wedges; serve very cold, each wedge topped with a large dollop of whipped cream.

Yield: 8 servings.

★ ★

The chickens have been in Key West for more than 175 years. Their numbers grew in the 1950s, when Cubans arrived en masse to staff the city's cigar factories. Raised for their meat, eggs, and fighting ability, the colorful, pugnacious fowl flew the coop and are now a plentiful, if not necessarily welcome, component of island life. Besides creating traffic hazards, the chickens tear up gardens; foul yards, cars, and roofs; and just generally make a noisy nuisance of themselves. The city government made several unsuccessful—and unpopular— attempts to deal with the problem, including one assistant city manager's suggestion that citizens wring their necks. A humane trapping and relocation system was eventually settled upon.

When we visited Key West, there were still plenty of hens and roosters strutting about and an equal number of tourists taking pictures of them.

Whatever your opinion of them, they are a colorful and bizarre aspect to a city where the colorful and bizarre are the norm rather than the exception.

For more information on the "gypsy" chickens of Key West, contact keywestchickens.com.

Pucker Up
Key West

On first sight—or bite—the Key lime is unlikely to bowl you over.

Unlike the larger Persian lime, its skin is mottled yellow, not shiny green. It's seedy and small, not much bigger than a walnut. And, most distinctively, its taste is puckeringly sour.

So why all the fuss about a gnarly little lime that makes your face turn inside out? Three words: Key lime pie.

The official dessert of Key West, Key lime pie is described by *A Gourmet's Guide* as "an American pie containing a lime-flavored custard topped with meringue." This is incredibly simplistic; the question of whipped cream versus meringue can get you into a Duval Street bar fight, let alone the correct composition of a graham-cracker crust.

★ ★

To be authentic, a Key lime pie must be made with the juice of real Key limes.
PHOTO COURTESY OF VISIT FLORIDA

Key limes were the standard of the world before Persian limes and other varieties came along. Aside from their other drawbacks (see above), Key limes are sensitive to cold and grow on thorny trees. But if you lived in a tropical climate, wanted a good source of vitamin C, and weren't afraid of pricked fingers, Key limes got the job done.

Key limes were grown commercially in southern Florida and the Keys until the 1926 hurricane wiped out the groves. Small-scale and backyard production continues, however, so it is still possible to find the main ingredient of Key lime pie. (Do not use bottled Key lime juice if you can avoid it. The taste is nothing like that of the real, fresh-squeezed thing.)

✶ ✶

Key lime pie became identified with Key West because of the Key's isolation. Before the railroad opened in 1912, fresh milk was hard to come by. Gail Borden's invention of sweetened condensed (canned) milk in 1859 solved the problem: It allowed you to make a custard pie without cooking it. The Key lime juice was so acidic that it curdled the milk and egg yolks, creating an instant filling. (Today's concerns about salmonella usually result in the pie being baked to an internal temperature of 160 degrees.)

Accompany this dessert with a cold glass of sweet iced tea, and you've got yourself a true slice of paradise.

A Farewell to Savings
Key West

One of Ernest Hemingway's wives (we can't remember which one; he had four) thought she would surprise the famous author by building him a swimming pool, the first on Key West.

There were only about a hundred things wrong with the idea, the most obvious of which were (1) Key West is basically a big chunk of coral, meaning workers had to chisel the 10-foot-deep pool by hand; (2) the Atlantic Ocean and/or Gulf of Mexico is available for swimming purposes about two blocks away; and (3) it was built in 1938 during the Great Depression, when money was scarce. The other ninety-seven reasons? It cost $20,000.

Hemingway was less than thrilled by the gift. In fact, he took a penny from his pocket and announced jokingly (ha-ha!) to his wife, "Here, take the last penny I've got!"

Papa then pressed the penny into wet cement near the pool, where it remains to this day. (The pool is behind the Hemingway House and is part of the tour.)

The Ernest Hemingway Home & Museum is located at 907 Whitehead Street in Key West and is open 365 days a year from 9:00 a.m. to 5:00 p.m. Admission is charged. Phone (305) 294-1136 or visit www.hemingwayhome.com.

★ ★

The End of the Line
Key West

It's ironic that one of the things that makes Key West so popular is the fact that it's so remote.

It's almost 800 miles from Pensacola, in the Panhandle, to Key West. Miami may look close on the map, but you've still got a lot of driving to do.

Over time, Key Westers, or Conchs (pronounced *Conks*) as they prefer to be called, have hosted pirates, presidents, authors, play-wrights, hippies, artists, the military, real estate speculators, and tour-ists. A Conch either learns to be tolerant or he moves someplace else.

In 1982, Key West threatened to secede from the United States. The locals intended to call themselves the Conch Republic. Yes, plenty of alcohol is consumed in Key West.

Today, tourists try to capture the cachet of the place by visiting Sloppy Joe's Saloon on Duval Street, a favorite hangout of Ernest Hemingway when he lived here from 1931 to 1961. They also have their picture taken by a thermos-bottle-shaped thing at the corner of South Street and Whitehead Street that marks the southernmost point in the continental United States. There's a painting of a conch shell at the top that reminds everyone that this is the Conch Republic; at the bottom, more lettering describes Key West as the "Home of the Sun Set."

Not nearly as ominous as the proximity of Havana, but, hey, it still makes a good picture.

Holy Jurassic Park, Batman! It's a Polydactyl!
Key West

It's rather sad that the first question people ask when they take the tour of the house of Ernest Hemingway, arguably America's most famous author, is "Where are the six-toed cats?"

★ ★

They don't want to know what inspired *To Have and Have Not,* where he wrote *For Whom the Bell Tolls,* or who the old man was in *The Old Man and the Sea.* What they want to know is where they can find the felines with the extra digits.

You don't have to look far. Of the sixty-one cats on the property, thirty-four are polydactyl, meaning they have more than the usual number of fingers or toes. (Since cats don't have fingers, we are talking, in this case, about toes.) Most have six toes, but four of the cats have seven. They don't seem to behave any differently from cats with the usual number of digits, although a few of them probably get tired of being gaped at by tourists.

Cats with extra toes were considered quite valuable in the old days, and Hemingway obtained his first polydactyl cat from a sea captain. Its name was Snowball (the cat's, not the sea captain's).

The cats did what cats are wont to do, and pretty soon the Hemingway property was awash (aspray?) with polydactyl kitties. Hemingway, for some reason known only to him, named his mutant cats after celebrities and movie stars. There was a cat named Bette Davis, one named Frank Sinatra, and another named Marilyn Monroe.

Our tour guide, Mark, said the genetic integrity of the seven generations of six-toed cats will never be in danger due to the territorial nature of the beasts. If a five-toed interloper hops the fence in hopes of contaminating the gene pool, he quickly encounters sixty-one Hemingway cats with other ideas.

It's all very interesting, we suppose, if you like cats, but we find the prospect of buying eighty pounds of cat food a week poly-ridiculous.

The Ernest Hemingway Home & Museum is located at 907 Whitehead Street. Phone (305) 294-1136 or visit www.hemingwayhome .com. Admission is charged. The house is open 365 days a year.

★ ★

Here Chick Chick
Key West

Katha Sheehan describes herself as a "defense attorney" for Key West's flocks of free-roaming chickens.

"Wild chickens have lived here for at least 200 years," said Sheehan, known locally as the Chicken Lady. "Pirates probably brought the first ones to use as fighting cocks; they're part of our history. People complain about the crowing and the way they scratch around in their gardens, but chickens do a lot of good, too."

Sheehan says the wild chickens, which number somewhere around 2,000, eat poisonous scorpions and centipedes, ticks, cockroaches, and termites. They are also a colorful—if somewhat noisy—symbol of Key West's laid-back, anything-goes lifestyle, she says.

The trouble is that the chickens act like they own the place, and that brings them into conflict with cars and bicycles, as well as homeowners who do not wish to be awakened by raucous crowing at 4:00 a.m. Sometimes the fowl are the victims of foul play, and when that happens the Chicken Lady takes the injured bird back to her part-souvenir-shop, part-animal-hospital, part-petting-zoo called The Chicken Store.

At any one time between three and seventy chickens might be rehabbing at The Chicken Store, and Sheehan, an animal lover and former (unsuccessful) candidate for mayor, wouldn't have it any other way. "Someone needs to stand up for the chickens," she said.

The threat of avian flu has some people worrying about the wisdom of allowing flocks of untended chickens to roam the city. To allay fears, Sheehan recently invited state poultry inspectors to check out her chickens for symptoms of the disease. All were given a clean bill of health.

When we last spoke to Sheehan, she was tending to a chicken and a rabbit that had grown up together. The rabbit went by the name of Adrian, and the chicken, much to Sheehan's chagrin, was named Barbie Q. Chicken.

"I don't care for that," she sniffed. "We prefer non-culinary chicken humor around here."

The Chicken Store's website is www.thechickenstore.com.

The Sun Also Rises, but It Also Sets, Too
Key West

Key West was once a haven for pirates. Over time, it began attracting drifters, gypsies, hippies, real estate speculators, and tourists.

The jury is still out on whether any of this is an improvement.

In any event, the one thing everyone has in common is an appreciation of Key West's gorgeous sunsets. In other parts of America, people might just look at the sky and say, "My, what a lovely sunset." But this is, after all, Key West, and any occasion, even the daily setting of the sun, is reason for a party.

The party takes place every evening (sun permitting) at Mallory Square, at the foot of Duval Street. Legend has it that the famous playwright Tennessee Williams, gin and tonic firmly in hand, initiated the tradition of applauding the setting sun. By the 1960s, the tradition had a name: Sunset Celebration. Certain people were of the opinion that if a gin and tonic was good, LSD must be better, and they gathered at the square to watch Atlantis rising out of the clouds at sunset.

Today the scene is bizarre enough without hallucinogens. The setting sun competes for the crowd's attention with street vendors, jugglers, sword swallowers, contortionists, magicians, musicians, acrobats, and maybe even the Ghost of Atlantis if atmospheric conditions are just right.

The party begins about two hours before sunset. Just follow the crowd.

Diary of a Hurricane
Long Key

The so-called Labor Day Hurricane of 1935 has the dubious distinction of being the most violent storm in American history.

With sustained winds of 200 miles per hour and gusts possibly exceeding 250 miles per hour (exact numbers are unavailable because all wind-measuring equipment was destroyed), the Labor Day hurricane killed 423 people in the Keys: 164 civilians and 259 World War I veterans staying in work camps while building US 1. Most victims drowned when an 18-foot wall of water surged over the low-lying Keys. Some were killed by flying debris; some were simply sandblasted to death.

J. E. Duane, an observer for the Weather Bureau, was in charge of a fishing camp on Long Key when the eye of the brutal Category 5 hurricane passed around 9:30 p.m. on September 2, 1935. Here is his account:

September 2:

2 p.m. Barometer falling; heavy sea swell and a high tide; heavy rain squalls continued. Wind from N. or NNE., force 6.

3 p.m. Ocean swells have changed; this change noted was that large waves were rolling in from SE., somewhat against winds which were still in N. or NE.

4 p.m. Wind still N., increasing to force 9. Barometer dropping 0.01 every five minutes. Rain continued.

5 p.m. Wind N., hurricane force. Swells from SE.

6 p.m. Barometer 28.04; still falling. Heavy rains. Wind still N.

6:45 p.m. Barometer 27.90. Wind backing to NW., increasing; plenty of flying timbers and heavy timber, too—seemed it made no difference as to weight and size. A beam 6 by 8 inches, about 18 feet long, was blown from north side of camp, about 300 yards, through observer's house, wrecking it and nearly striking 3 persons. Water 3 feet deep from top of railroad grade, or about 16 feet.

★ ★

7 p.m. We are now located in main lodge building of camp; flying timbers have now begun to wreck this lodge, and it is shaking on every blast. Water has now reached level of railway on north side of camp.

9 p.m. No signs of storm letting up. Barometer still falling very fast.

9:20 p.m. Barometer 27.22 inches; wind abated. We now hear other noises than the wind and know center of storm is over us. Heading now for last and only cottage that I think can or will stand the blow due to arrive shortly. All hands, 20 in number, gather in this

PHOTO COURTESY OF VISIT FLORIDA

cottage. During this lull the sky is clear to northward. Stars shining brightly and a very light breeze continues; no flat calm. About the middle of the lull, which lasted a timed 55 minutes, the sea began to lift up, it seemed, and rise very fast; this from ocean side of camp. I put my flashlight out on sea and could see walls of water which seemed many feet high. I had to race fast to regain entrance to cottage, but water caught me waist-deep, although water was

The Old Man and the Urinal

Six-toed cats may or may not be your thing, but there are other reasons to visit Ernest Hemingway's house.

Take urinals, for instance.

Papa Hemingway spent a lot of time in Sloppy Joe's Saloon on Duval Street. Tourists flock there to this day, hoping that the consumption of sufficient quantities of margaritas will inspire them to write the Great American Novel. (America is still waiting.)

Anyway, Hemingway and the urinal in Sloppy Joe's men's room formed a relationship, of sorts, to the point that when Hemingway bought his house on Whitehead Street, he decided to bring the bathroom fixture along with him.

Today the urinal serves as a drinking fountain for the home's sixty-one cats. None of them, to our knowledge, has written the Great American Novel either.

A urinal from Sloppy Joe's Saloon is now a water fountain for cats at the Hemingway House.

only about 60 feet from doorway of cottage. Water lifted cottage from its foundations, and it floated.

10:10 p.m. The first blast from SSW., full force. House now breaking up—winds seems stronger than any time during storm. I glanced at the barometer which read 26.98 inches, dropped it in water and was blown outside to sea; got hung up in broken fronds of

★ ★

coconut tree and hung on for dear life. I was then struck by some object and knocked unconscious.

September 3:

2:25 a.m. I became conscious in tree and found I was lodged about 20 feet above ground. All water had disappeared from island; the cottage had been blown back on the island, from whence the sea receded and left it with all people safe.

A Gastropod by Any Other Name

It is not unreasonable to ask why residents of Key West wish to be referred to as a marine snail.

A conch (pronounced *conk*) is a type of whelk, the queen conch, and also a lifelong resident of Key West. (A bartender informed us that people who have lived in Key West a minimum of seven years now qualify as conchs. Standards continue to deteriorate.)

Why conchs? Well, they are, or were, a staple of a Key Wester's diet. The chewy meat is/was eaten raw (ugh!) or marinated in vinegar for salad. Conch is fried to make conch steak, diced to make conch fritters, or stewed as part of conch chowder (yum!).

Conchs (the sea-critter variety) were eventually overharvested to the point that all Florida conch meat now comes from the Bahamas. That is fitting because some say the first conchs (the human variety) were British sympathizers during Revolutionary War days who hid in the Bahamas after announcing that they'd rather go to war than eat conch. (Many tourists, upon tasting rubbery conch meat for the first time, have made the same vow.) When Florida became a territory of

★ ★

Hurricane winds continued till 5 a.m. and during this period terrific lightning flashes were seen. After 5 a.m. strong gales continued throughout the day with heavy rain.

A stone monument to the victims of the 1935 Labor Day hurricane can be found on Islamorada at Mile Marker 82 on the oceanside. Called the Florida Keys Memorial, the monument is made of native keystone and bears a frieze depicting coconut palms bending in the

the United States in 1821, Bahamians involved in the salvage industry moved to the Keys and brought the conch label with them.

Another theory suggests that conchs are called conchs because they used to eat a lot of the once prolific critters and used the empty shells as signaling trumpets.

Whatever the origin of the word, it is considered a good thing to be a conch. In the old days, families would put a conch shell on a stick to announce the birth of a baby. Today, city officials declare someone an "official conch" if he or she does something praiseworthy of a civic nature, and new residents are referred to as "freshwater conchs."

Derived from the Greek word meaning "shell," the conch's Latin name is *Strombus gigas*. This, thankfully, is not a well-known fact, which explains why the Key West tourist conveyance is called the Conch Train, Key West High School sports teams are referred to as the Fighting Conchs, and the cheerleading squad is called the Conchettes.

"Go fighting *Strombus gigas*!" would simply not do as a school cheer, particularly on third and long.

hurricane winds while an angry sea laps at the bottom of their trunks. In 1937, the cremated remains of 300 victims were placed within the tiled crypt in front of the monument.

If You Build It, They Won't Necessarily Come
Sugarloaf Key

Of all the batty ideas, this one has to be the battiest.

Richter Clyde Perky was one of the biggest landowners in the Florida Keys in the 1920s. He founded a town on Sugarloaf Key called, unimaginatively enough, Perky. The centerpiece of the town was a fancy fishing resort to which wealthy tourists from New York and other points north were transported aboard Henry Flagler's new Overseas Railroad to Key West.

The resort had everything a vacationer might want: a lodge, guest cottages, a restaurant, and a fully equipped marina. Unfortunately, it also had something every vacationer didn't want: swarms and swarms of relentless, blood-sucking mosquitoes.

South Florida was mosquito heaven in those days. Locals pretty much accepted them as a fact of life, but tourists were not so forgiving, and business at the lodge dried up faster than a Yankee in Bermuda shorts.

But Perky was not about to be beaten by a lowly insect. He began reading a book titled *Bats, Mosquitoes, and Dollars*. Bats, he learned, love to eat mosquitoes. Perky loved dollars. He learned to love bats.

After contacting the book's author, Dr. Charles A. R. Campbell, Perky began construction of a giant bat roost in March 1929. The 30-foot-high unpainted wooden tower was built behind what is now Sugarloaf Lodge at a cost of $10,000. The stubby, shingled pyramid with a louvered door to allow the bats in and out sits on four legs and looks a little like an unfinished wooden rocket ship waiting to take off.

Perky might as well have tried flying it to the moon, because the bat house never attracted a single bat.

This puzzled Perky, because he had seen bats flitting about Sugarloaf Key in the evening. Why were they turning up their noses at his house?

The Perky Bat House on Sugarloaf Key never solved the island's mosquito problem, but it sure did exude some out-of-this-world aromas.

For answers, Perky again contacted Dr. Campbell. After some thought, Dr. Campbell decided what the bat tower needed was bat bait. What are the ingredients of bat bait? Oh, just everyday things you've probably got lying around the house. Things like bat guano and ground-up sex organs of female bats. Mix it all together and you have something that Perky's right-hand man, Fred L. Johnson, said smelled "like nothing on earth."

★ ★

You would think that bats would come from miles around to wallow in something as aromatic as Dr. Campbell's special bat bait. But the bats of Sugarloaf Key were apparently fussier than most, and they continued to stay away in droves.

Time passed. The bat bait, aged by heat and humidity, went from smelling like nothing on earth to smelling like nothing in the solar system or even nearby galaxies. Still no bats, although occasionally a passing bird would be knocked unconscious by the stink and fall from the sky. We're making that last part up. We think.

Today, the Perky Bat House is as batless as ever, but Monroe County Mosquito Control's insecticide sprays have, too late for Richter Clyde Perky, finally solved the problem of mosquitoes on Sugarloaf Key.

So the story has a happy ending, in a batty sort of way.

The Perky Bat House is located behind Sugarloaf Key Lodge at Mile Marker 17. Turn at the tennis courts, and it's down a dirt road about a quarter of a mile.

index

★ ★

index

index

about the authors

★ ★

David Grimes is a humor writer based in Bradenton, Florida. He lives in a heavily mortgaged house that he shares with his wife, Teri, and two incontinent pugs.

Tom Becnel writes feature stories and an outdoor recreation column called "Go!" for the *Sarasota Herald-Tribune.* He lives in Port Charlotte with his wife, Naomi, and daughters Audrey and Marie—the "Go!" girls.